# The SIMPLE ART of GREATNESS

*Building, Managing and Motivating a Kick-Ass Workforce*

# *The* SIMPLE ART *of* GREATNESS

James X Mullen

VIKING

VIKING
Published by the Penguin Group
Penguin Books USA Inc., 375 Hudson Street, New York, New York 10014, U.S.A.
Penguin Books Ltd, 27 Wrights Lane, London W8 5TZ, England
Penguin Books Australia Ltd, Ringwood, Victoria, Australia
Penguin Books Canada Ltd, 10 Alcorn Avenue,
Toronto, Ontario, Canada M4V 3B2
Penguin Books (N.Z.) Ltd, 182–190 Wairau Road,
Auckland 10, New Zealand

Penguin Books Ltd, Registered Offices: Harmondsworth, Middlesex, England

First published in 1995 by Viking Penguin, a division of Penguin Books USA Inc.

1  3  5  7  9  10  8  6  4  2

Grateful acknowledgment is made for permission to use the following copyrighted works: Number Seventeen from "The Way of Life According to Laotzu" from *The Chinese Translations* by Witter Bynner. Copyright © 1944 by Witter Bynner and copyright renewed © 1972 by Dorothy Chauvenet and Paul Horgan. Reprinted by permission of Farrar, Straus & Giroux, Inc. Adaptation of "Owners Need Not Apply" by James X. Mullen. Used with permission from *Inc.* magazine, August 1990. Copyright 1990 by Goldhirsh Group, Inc., 38 Commercial Wharf, Boston, MA 02110. Excerpt from "The Green Isle in the Sea" from *Fables for Our Time* by James Thurber, published by Harper & Row. Copyright © 1940 James Thurber. Copyright © 1968 Helen Thurber. By permission of James Thurber Literary Properties.

library of congress cataloging in publication data
Mullen, James X.
The simple art of greatness: building, managing
and motivating a kick-ass workforce/by James X. Mullen.
p.  cm.
ISBN 0–670–85211–2
1. Employee motivation.  2. Personnel management.
3. Entrepreneurship. I. Title.
HF5549.5.M63M85    1995
658.3—dc20    94–31390

This book is printed on acid-free paper. ∞

Printed in the United States of America
Set in Goudy

This book is dedicated to four inspiring teachers:
my cousin John P. McGrail, Brother Ricardo CFX,
Dr. Bert L. Vallee, and E. Hyde Cox;
and to the men and women who built
and sustain our agency.

"A company, like so many other things in life, is not something you inherit or take over from your predecessors. It is something you borrow from future generations."

—Bernd Pischetsrieder

Chairman of the Board, BMW AG

Frankfurt Motor Show

September 7, 1993

# $\mathscr{P}$REFACE

BOOKS ARE HARD, but book titles are fun. When required by a grade-school teacher to editorialize on a subject that would command a reader's interest, I titled my essay: *How to Cut and Shrink a Human Head*. Our local librarian was very helpful with my research, but she kept me away from her cat.

By college, I had begun to muse on a tongue-in-cheek handle for the autobiography I never intend to write, settling finally on *You Pray, I'll Shoot*—a personal philosophy that has guided my entire life, and that I continue to espouse to this day. In some distant decade, I suppose, I'll find myself with either too much time or too little money and will yield to the temptation to produce an exposé of advertising's deepest secrets. True to the hyperbolic nature of my profession, I'll call that book *Everything I Know About Advertising, and More.*

While the title of this slim volume was less whimsically considered, it is, if anything, even more vulnerable to the healthy skepticism of the real-life men and women struggling to get along in the everyday business world. Yes, I recognize that *The Simple Art of Greatness* smacks of arch moral authority, and that it pretentiously promises to deliver a monumental virtue with seductive ease. You would not be the first to raise this skeptical perspective. As one friend put it when I originally floated out the title, "Jim, you are making smart people the grandest business promise since Communism!

"Let me see if I've got this right," my associate continued. "Greatness made simple? Philosophies that translate into career moves? Are you really asking intelligent adults to spend time and money on a book by an unknown author on the chance he might actually know something that will change the courses of their businesses as well as, not incidentally, their whole lives?"

Well, umm . . . in short, yes, both. I believe with all my heart that the philosophies and practices used to create what

I describe as "a kick-ass workforce" can in fact become the engines of success in any business, regardless of its character, nature, size, scope, or dimension. Forcefully applied, these simple principles will inject a splash of nitro to the quiescent glycerin of a promise-packed entrepreneurial business; artfully exercised, they have the power to galvanize a mid-size company into regaining its vigor and toughness; and judiciously implemented, they even can catalyze very large organizations—departmentally and corporately—by blasting away those carbuncular layers of bureaucratic ennui that drag down both employee morale and bottom-line profitability.

How can I be so Jesuitically certain of these statements? To be sure, I see the effect these principles have had in building Mullen, an agency that I believe is respected and that I know to be profitable. But more than that, I've witnessed these principles operating—sometimes in full howl, sometimes merely in transcendental glimmers—in every truly successful organization I've ever encountered. And when doubters tell me these simple concepts won't work in large companies, won't survive the crush of huge revenue volumes or the geographical extensions of a corporate giant, I suggest they talk with Dr. Bob Beyster, chairman of the $1.7 billion Science Applications International Corporation. The company Bob founded is now owned by its 17,000 employees and does most of its business with the U.S. government, for goodness' sake! Yet its vigor and spirit make SAIC a soul mate to our agency, which, in people and billings, is a fraction of its size.

As you've probably gathered by now, the simple principles that build business greatness are not another laundry list of organizational do's and don'ts, but a new and all-encompassing business *attitude*, core concepts to be carried around in your heart that will equip you to engage whatever unique problems plague your department, your company or your industry. As often as possible, I hope to ground these principles with specific management practices that will apply as productively to the manufacture of computers or ladies' hats as they do in my own field of advertising. With luck, they will have the same effect on you as the teachings and wisdom of the noted Italian chef and author Marcella Hazan have had on my wife's cooking skills (and, therefore, indirectly on the splendor of our family dinners).

At the classes Marcella holds both in Venice's fresh food markets and her own apartment kitchen, this inspiring chef doesn't teach her students how to perfect complex recipes; she teaches them to understand food. As Marcella observes, "If you don't have all the ingredients for a dish you're cooking, what are you going to do, run out and go shopping?" (Ah, well, Marcella . . . I mean, most of us always have.)

To those like Marcella who understand food, a recipe is not a dictate, it's a concept. Once this concept is internalized, then whatever is fresh and best in the market that day determines the final menu, and whatever supporting ingredients are already on hand define the style of preparation. The original recipe is merely a historical reference to what others have found successful, not a format to be followed slavishly.

Similarly, if I can leave you armed with a few truly fundamental principles and help you infuse these concepts into your everyday work environment, you'll notice the differences almost immediately. And if you can teach these same principles to other managers in your organization, then, world, watch out!

All that being said, I confess that it feels a little weird (and more than a little presumptuous) for a man who tries to be intellectually honest to offer with confidence a book on business management that truly supplies its readers a road map to greatness. I am poignantly aware that it took our agency twenty-five wretchedly long years to top $150 million in annual billings—in a world where hot high-tech companies hit those numbers before the first day's lunch. Worse yet, I confess to you that it took us that quarter century because I made (and remade) each mistake against which I caution herein, and was brutally punished for every one of them. It gives me some satisfaction to think that, if I may paraphrase a sports cliché, my pain may result in your gain.

Over the past few years, I've had the chance to test people's interest in these philosophies when speaking before executives at regional and national gatherings, as well as at large creative conferences sponsored by the advertising industry journal *Adweek*. In doing so, I've learned two things:

(1) Many, many people, especially creative professionals who are reputed to care nothing about business, are deeply offended and discouraged by the structures that characterize most of the companies where they work;

(2) I'm not the only CEO who's discovered this; in fact, an

encouraging number of business leaders recognize the problems and are themselves working on management solutions—some along parallel lines to those I suggest.

Therefore, since no great concept in this world is arrived at uninfluenced and with total originality, it should not be surprising that a goodly number of my messianic business philosophies and practices may feel familiar to managers who have encountered the same situations or traveled similar paths.

My particular theories have been drawn from thousands of personal experiences but, more important, from a handful of great teachers, some of whom you will meet anecdotally in these pages. In truth, most of the best stuff in this book began as other people's ideas. My excuse and hope is that this repackaging of universal principles will be sufficiently interesting and stimulating that *The Simple Art of Greatness* will make a difference in how each reader manages his or her organization, and in the business success and personal happiness that result.

I urge you to treat this book as a Fanny Farmer sampler: embrace the possibility that there's something philosophically worthwhile inside every theory, experience, or tip; but poke at the bottom of each to check out its specific relevance to you.

One person's taste for nougat is offset by another's yen for walnut cream.

Greatness isn't just simple. It's sweet.

P.S. THE CONTINUOUS USE of "his or her" to degenderize the third person singular will rapidly become tiring to both of us. May I have your permission to use "his" or "her" randomly throughout the rest of the book, thereby obviating this lumpy convention and skewering the even clumsier requirement of monotonously presenting the world in the plural? Thank you.

# $\mathscr{A}$CKNOWLEDGMENTS

THIS ENTIRE BOOK is a summary of others' contributions, but a few people deserve particular recognition and appreciation for their hands-on efforts.

Doe Coover, agent deluxe, taught me the rubrics of proposal development and provided the credibility of taste and judgment that helped persuade Viking to consider publication. Executive Editor Pam Dorman championed the project from the beginning, then gently eased me through the realities and difficulties of converting a concept into printed paper. Once the structure was in place, Pam's associate Carolyn Carlson did her best to straighten its wandering logic, filter out the murkier ideas, and control my natural tendency toward bombast. The flaws that remain can be traced directly to my author's ego.

The toughest reviews, however, occurred as my colleague and ally Katie Greenler reduced a messy pile of scribbles to an orderly manuscript, then refrained from braining me through fifty revisions. Katie's arched eyebrow is mightier than most editors' red pencils. Other early encouragement and harassment was offered by Margie Brandfon, who, because she hates the term "special thanks," receives mine. The elegant book jacket was a collaboration between two of our most talented professionals: Associate Creative Director Margaret McGovern and Graphics Specialist Judy Barolak. Viking's Neil Stuart provided production recommendations that made their design sing.

Perhaps the most valuable assistance I received was the tolerance of my wife, Nola, and that of my agency compatriots. They not only put up with my many idiosyncrasies and obsessions, they abet them.

All who contributed have my heart.

# CONTENTS

# *The* SIMPLE ART *of* GREATNESS

# I

## *A*N EPIPHANOUS MOMENT

BACK IN 1975, when the earth was still cooling and our tiny agency boasted four souls and billed less than a million dollars, I hired Steve Haesche, the first person I ever met who'd actually worked in the advertising business. In fact, Steve had been an art director at two very good agencies, one in New York, the second in Boston, where he had been something of a young star. True to his indomitable integrity (then and now), Steve opted for self-respect over glory by quitting his agency and taking a job cutting sails on the floor of a Marblehead loft—nights! I quickly learned that Steve had bailed out of the communications business because he hated advertising—not the process of making ads but the suffocating realities of being part of an exploitative industry.

I couldn't figure it out. For me, advertising fulfilled its apocryphal description of being "the most fun you can have with your clothes on." So one day after we had worked together for a while, I cornered Steve to try to uncover the source of his cynicism.

"You know, I'm happy for you, Jim," Steve began; "you've got a nice little agency, we're doing good work, and everyone's having fun. But if you ever realize your dream and this place grows up into something, I won't be here to see it. One of these years we'll have a problem or get stiffed for a lot of money or lose a big account—something. You'll look around to see how you can cut costs so the company can survive and you'll figure out that, after four or five years of pay raises, I could be replaced by a hot young kid for half the money.

"But of course, if I do what I have to do for myself, I'll be out of here before you get the chance to get rid of me. Once or twice every few months, I'll be packing up my portfolio and pretending to be on a photo shoot while I'm really out interviewing at some other agencies. In this industry, changing jobs is about the only way to keep my income going up and stay a jump ahead of the layoffs.

"Besides, I've learned that what I get paid has nothing to

do with how I contribute. I get paid on how badly management thinks they need me. It's just that, with every year that goes by, I'll be getting more and more scared, knowing that I've got a family and that they're relying on me to provide them with a normal life.

"But you know, no matter what I do I'm screwed, because I can't help getting older. Sooner or later I'll be with an agency that loses an account, and no matter how I scramble, I'll get laid off one more time. Then some young kid art director will make a funny good-bye card for me, just like I've done lots of times for other old guys on their way out, and everyone will go down to some trendy advertising bar and get drunk—and I'll be gone.

"Now what? Who wants to hire a fifty-year-old art director? By that time I'll have kids in college and no money to keep them there. I suppose I'll own a house and maybe a boat, but that will be it. I'll probably have to sell both to keep going.

"Jim," Steve concluded, "for me this business is a dilemma. It's what I do best—but it's also what's going to kill me."

Whew! I thought about what Steve had said and knew in my heart that he was right, about a lot of things. Of all the businesses that have institutionalized employee disloyalty, advertising leads the pack. Our industry's employee practices are as destructive as Steve made them out to be. We habitually put our best people on career roller coasters, pampering our stars-of-the-moment with obscene largesse at times of great agency updrafts, then abruptly firing the very same people when the corporate need for reduced payroll outstrips the value of their contributions. Sad to say, even the smart ones get so caught up in the trappings of success that they're slow to realize how their sudden stature and earnings can ebb as rapidly as they flowed. When this apocalypse happens (as it almost inevitably will for all who are not protected by the security of significant agency ownership), it is followed by the stigma of public failure and a desperate, sometimes fearful, attempt to maintain an unrealistically pumped-up standard of living. What a horrible thing to do to the very people whose skills and talent were the muscle and sinew that built the company.

In fact, that painful conversation with Steve Haesche truly changed my life. Our agency stopped being just a business dedicated to creating great advertising and became an organization equally dedicated to the pursuit of a great quality of life for all who would build it.

I consider myself extremely fortunate to have learned this lesson relatively early in our company's history, when the costs of change were slight. But what astonishes me most is that most of the leaders of our largest industries have never figured out the same thing. Our American workers are the grandchildren of immigrants, people bold enough to leave the stifling status-quo societies of Europe and Asia, who with nothing more than hands and hearts built the greatest country in modern times. These employees are the cultural descendants of families who pushed west in wagons, vulnerable to everything except defeat. They are the spiritual heirs of the cowboys, inventors, railroad builders, war winners, and space explorers. Why, then, do the majority of American businesses treat them like idiots?

I am convinced that American workers are culturally, genetically, endemically ambitious. They are born energetic and raised to be competitive. Their heroes and heroines aren't institutions, they're strong and independent individuals— sports, film, and real-life people who cut wide swaths through life. Young Americans enter the workforce brimming with pride and eager for accomplishment. It is only when beaten down by the twin corrupters of individualism—insensitive bottom-line management and lowest-common-denominator standards—that they react with self-protective timidity, lethargy, and disloyalty.

It is my passionate belief that the safest, most efficient way a company can achieve its full potential is by making its workforce powerful enough to be dangerous. Individual by individual, it must cede its employees enough authority to make them great—to define and build their own jobs, to speak for and commit to their companies, to create a productive environment with high community standards and to lead happy, civilized lives.

# 2

# $\mathcal{O}$RIGINS

THERE IS A SAYING in the Middle East that applies as readily to authors as it does to Persian rugs: "Before you judge the fiber of the carpet, judge the fiber of the man selling it to you." By that logic, you have a right to gauge the quality of the following chapters by first testing the tensility of my personal autobiographical threads.

Therefore, now is probably a good time for me to acknowledge that my views toward business have been defined by the cumulative experiences of a rather nonlinear life. At a minimum, your awareness of this broken-field dash toward business enlightenment will diminish your bafflement at the disparateness of the references and anecdotes that salt these pages. At a maximum, it will support my premise that a variety of hands-on experiences yields lessons that transfer readily from one situation to another, as opposed to stiff, impractical graduate school theories that never quite answer real-life problems. Also, as a dubious bonus, this tale of good times and high adventure will give all the kids in your family fabulous arguments for ignoring parental pleas to get on with responsible careers and, instead, encourage them to emulate my virtual post-graduate retirement. Ergo, here is *You Pray, I'll Shoot,* the Cliffs Notes version.

It was my good fortune to grow up in America in the forties and fifties, an era of confident prosperity and surefooted family values. The first twenty years were spent in a Massachusetts mill town named Clinton, which by college I had relabeled Apathy. (Yes, I'd assure Midwestern girls, Apathy is located right there outside of Worcester, nestled comfortably among Doldrum, Lassitude, Indifference, and Ennui.) Clinton, Massachusetts was all white, heavily Irish, mostly Catholic, thoroughly middle class and unceasingly colorful. Locals of earlier generations had nicknames like "Butsy," "Bibbers," "Nummy," and "Boogers" and were addressed as such, by adults and kids alike, with dignity.

Given the town, the time and my family's modest finances,

it seemed quite normal to study nine years locally with the Presentation nuns and then four years in Worcester with the Xaverian Brothers in inexorable preparation for matriculation with the Jesuits at Holy Cross. Originally I aspired to a career in medicine, less for the profession's nobility than because I always liked nice cars. (In my hometown, only the doctors drove Packards.) Ah, but college opened my educational horizons, and, while I continued to major in the physical sciences, my heart lined up behind painting, poetry, literature and music. Since there were no limits on the number of courses a Holy Cross student in that era could take, I often signed up for thirty-five to forty hours of class and lab each semester, close to double the going schedule. Good thing, too. After cutting (and failing) an entire semester's lab duties in a required Organic Chemistry course, our generous school president reconfigured my bizarre glut of extra credits to formulate a degree never offered at Holy Cross before or since: a Bachelor of Science in Fine Arts. (As the president, Fr. Swords, commented in a letter accompanying the sheepskin he mailed to my mother, ". . . and I do recognize the contradiction.")

My declining interest in the world's duodena made art school an inviting postgraduate alternative to medical school, although not a very popular choice at home. "I see, Jim," my mother coolly observed, "you've decided not to become a doctor. You've decided to be a bum." While the poor lady had a point, I've never regretted the outcome of that pivotal choice.

After a few restless semesters at Boston's School of the Museum of Fine Arts, I youthfully concluded that it was my duty, obligation and mission to invent American painting, choosing for its nascence the Greek island of Rhodes. Well, perhaps this decision wasn't driven entirely by painterly dreams, as Rhodes is, perhaps, the most temperate and romantic of the entire Cycladic chain. There in true artistic fashion I drew, I painted, I read, and I starved. For food and lodging, I taught English to the island's chief military officer by enticing him to read Oscar Wilde aloud. (Astonishingly, he never questioned my choice of authors and, in the process, also educated me. "Heliotrope," he'd somberly explain as I struggled for a simple way to describe that color, "is a Greek word.")

My own bookish pursuits were the cultural reciprocal—Homer's *Iliad* and *Odyssey*—devoured while leaning on the Doric columns on an acropolis bordering the loud-sounding

Aegean, watching the rosy-fingered dawn illuminate the wine-dark sea.

After surviving the better part of a year in Europe on my wits and about two hundred dollars, I retreated to Boston, stone broke and a little lonely, equipped with my sole quasi-commercial skill: good technique in a science laboratory. That background and my ability to interpret scientific principles in cartoon form landed me a job at the Harvard Biophysics Research Lab. By day I operated spectrographs, prowling for traces of zinc in the metalo-enzyme liver alcohol dehydrogenase; by night I drew slide shows for the lab chief's lectures.

Just as my family brightened with hope that I was trending toward a level of normalcy their friends could respect, I was once again rescued from regular employment by my then (and still) fatal preference for the word "yes." I accepted a friend's invitation to help him and his wife outfit their quirky thirty-five-foot cutter, a blunt old throwback to the era of British sailing trawlers, and to sail it from Southampton, England, to the Virgin Islands, by way of Spain, Portugal, Madeira, the Canaries, and Antigua. The penultimate leg, thirty-two days across the southern Atlantic, was mostly boring, partly terrifying, and entirely monkishly spiritual. But when we made our landfall in English Harbor, I thought I had sailed into heaven, and I saw absolutely no good reason to leave the simple, lovely islands of the Caribbean ever again. Cold weather, science, and respectability were no match for blandishments of splendid old yachts, bountiful rum, turquoise anchorages, and the busy companionship available to a charter boat captain.

Yet I learned in the Caribbean that an unchallenged life is something akin to a warm bath: richly indulgent when you first sink in, but rapidly turning tepid and, ultimately, maddeningly boring.

Days for most charter skippers began at 9:00 A.M. with an eye-opener at Fearless Fred Flotman's dockside bar and continued with rum and tonic restoratives until normal functionality ceased. By the age of forty, most of the charter operators had "swallowed the anchor," as we colorfully and nautically described the high incidence of alcoholism. Me? I was above that stuff. At twenty-five, I never took a drink before noon!

After a few seasons in this numbing paradise, a sense of survival prompted me to return to splash around the sober New England waters as skipper of a corporate yacht, a nice little Alden owned by a sailboat hardware manufacturer. But New England has these things called seasons, so, at summer's end, I found myself transferred to the company's customer service department, where I got to see corporate America in action (and inaction) for the first time. More excitingly, through the influence of a fellow sailor in the engineering department, I discovered the salty thrills of offshore yacht racing.

After several confusing and discouraging years in what proved to be a fetid corporate culture (more later), I plotted my escape. Operating on the Willie Sutton principle of opportunity, I decided to seek work where ocean racing was most available—sailmaker Ted Hood's loft in charming and historic Marblehead, Massachusetts. Ted's customers needed motivated crews as much as they needed fast boats, which allowed me to make my living selling sails while racing across many of the seven seas. In short order I became something of an oceangoing game of squash. By saying yes to every customer's invitation to race and by returning home from each trip with a fistful of orders, I was able to sail as many as eighty to ninety days a year.

When, in 1970, Ted sold his business, I had the inspired fantasy to open up an advertising agency. After all, I had written all my life, spent two years in art school and, after a fashion, run an in-house agency at Hood Sailmakers. Besides, advertising is one of the few professions that doesn't require a license, capital equipment or even seed money. Any creatively ambitious soul armed with no more than a pen, a pad of paper, and a paid-up telephone bill can instantly anoint himself a legitimate professional.

My motivation for starting my own business was entirely venal: I wanted to raise enough money to build a boat and attempt a circumnavigation of the world. To my astonishment, however, while entrepreneurism began as an ember, its health, growth and stature quickly blazed to become the consuming passion of my life. For all of the struggles and heartaches of those early years, they taught me what many before already had learned: business, not racing, is the ultimate sport.

Sometime in the mid-seventies, my sea legs turned to rubber and I retired from offshore sailboats, determined to drop out of racing completely—except, perhaps, among the enthusiasts who competed casually in vintage automobiles. For many years I had been tracing rumors to old barns in search of

1950s race cars that nobody wanted (but I did). For me, the attraction of vintage cars was less for their on-track potential than because they were visually arresting kinetic sculptures, powerful expressions of automotive art. At my high water mark, I had exhumed and owned as many as twenty-seven—Ferraris, Coopers, BMWs, McLarens, Brabhams, and Lotuses (Loti?) as well as sundry odds and ends with obscure names like Lister, Bristol, Elva, and Abarth.

Under the skilled hands of my friend, employee and brilliant craftsman Jay Dow (a personal mechanic being life's ultimate luxury), most of these cars were restored to functional perfection but allowed to remain cosmetically in tatty veteran condition. As time passed, many became quite valuable. Jay once described the Ferrari Short Wheelbase Berlinetta that I raced in the infamous and illegal Cannonball Run as the only million-dollar car he needed a tetanus shot to work on.

As Jay prepared a series of ever-faster vintage race cars, I joined an eclectic clique of old-guys-who-pretend on a Walter Mitty racing circuit. If I once considered sailing to be the sport of kings, then kings can't afford to race cars. Unbeknownst to me, I had stumbled into a competitive arena that has made many an enthusiast's bankruptcy possible. ("I know there's money in car racing," said one former multimillionaire, "because I *put* it there!") After a few years of vintage competition, I began to race more earnestly, in quick, demanding little open-wheel cars called Formula Fords. With a modicum of skill and an avalanche of good luck, I moved from Formula Fords to sports racers, and through the amateur ranks to steady drives with professional teams running Mazdas and then Porsches. In 1983 our team won both The 12 Hours of Sebring and the IMSA series GTO championships. Ultimately, with ten wins in GTU and GTO cars, I graduated to the winged 210+ mph racing Batmobiles called GT Prototypes, then the fastest cars in the world.

In 1986 a high-speed crash in a Buick-powered March prototype left my codriver, John Kalagian, a quadriplegic and left me significantly more contemplative. Besides, I was approaching my fifties, and to my astonishment, our agency was emerging as a national creative player in the advertising field. The choice became obvious. It turned out that not only was business the ultimate sport, it was also the one in which I had the best potential for long-term success.

Strange as it may seem, all of these seemingly unassociated

experiences in schools, travel, laboratories, boats, and race cars combined to teach me a great deal about running an organization. If a common thread could be traced, it was that each required independent thinking and a willingness to rely on trusted associates. Collectively, these seemingly unrelated activities trained me to be a strong individual within competent teams—lessons to be wrapped in tissues of gold.

Nearly four decades ago, while I was in prep school, an early mentor named Brother Ricardo compared the learning experience to the installation of mental hooks on which the student could spend a life hanging associated knowledge. Retrospectively, I came to realize that science, traveling, sailing, adventuring, car racing and entrepreneurism all provided a mind full of hooks, each gathering experiences that have translated into the purposeful business philosophies and irregular operating practices that make up this book.

So, then, is messing around a fair substitute for an MBA? Perhaps not for everyone, but it was for me. While graduate schools may provide their share of information hooks for earnest students, I prejudicially believe that academically acquired business knowledge remains just that—academic. I stand convinced that learning by passionate living will always yield a defining advantage over even the best of bookish degrees.

Besides, judging by my experiences, flat-out living is a lot more fun than graduate school.

# 3

## *W*HY A GREAT COMPANY?

M O S T   P E O P L E who've been propelled into management
slots arrive with a clear grasp of the concept that businesses
must make money. Yet no matter how passionately this goal is
reinforced, management's insistence on profit provides no
strategy for actually achieving it.

Managers in a *great* company start in a completely different place. Instead of targeting an acceptable profit margin and
creating schemes and budgets that will yield this bottom line
number, great company managers first define their qualitative
objectives and then implement strategies that will motivate
their employees to reach for excellence. *The entire premise of
this book hinges on the concept that the most reliable way to achieve
long term profitability is to create long term employee relationships*

*based on fairness, loyalty, and trust.* Not only will these seemingly altruistic principles make the organization quantitatively more successful, they will add the immeasurable benefit of making the entire workforce—employees and managers—significantly happier.

Bucks through happiness? Too squishy a concept for you? Too ephemeral a business objective to be practical? Allow me, please, to give you a brutally concrete example of the power of qualitative management over quantitative administration; of aspirational philosophies over regulatory policies; of distributed trust over centralized control.

Let me begin by taking you back to the palmy days of March 1987, when our company, along with most of the country, was enjoying good times and high prosperity. We then had sixty-five employees, annual billings of $46 million, and had edged into the ranks of America's top 150 largest advertising agencies. Our client roster was blue chip, bristling with legendary brands like Boston Whaler, Maserati, Puma, Stride-Rite, Dun & Bradstreet Software, and Apollo computers. And if our representation of Fortune 500 companies was minimal, our recognition among our peers in the advertiser community was absolutely incandescent. Through a sizable collection of awards for creative excellence, we had become one of our industry's emerging darlings.

In those heavy years of business adolescence, the physical expression of our agency's financial success (as well as its corporate quirkiness) was its unusual location and its unusually magnificent facility. We had always operated outside of Boston and a year earlier had purchased and remodeled twenty-five thousand square feet of elegant space in Prides Crossing, crown jewel of Massachusetts' toney North Shore. The estate had previously belonged to the newspaper magnate Bill Loeb and reflected both his wealth and taste. Its long, sinuous driveway wound through ninety acres of forested land to our hilltop headquarters, the renovated and expanded Loeb mansion, which commanded the highest shoreline peak between Boston and New Hampshire. Nearly every office was blessed with 180-degree ocean vistas scanning Massachusetts Bay from Marblehead to Gloucester. Our conference rooms seemed to float above a sea of pines whose treetops feathered into the watery blue of distant Atlantic horizons.

Business was absolutely terrific! We had been growing at over 40 percent cumulatively throughout the first seven years of the eighties, and had been routinely achieving profits consistent with the best in our industry. I thought that nothing could stop us, but I was wrong. On March 31, 1987, fate contrived to deliver our agency a devastating physical and financial blow, testing the viability of a management system threatened with potentially mortal consequences.

In the space of one violent day, a rogue fire tore through our building burning our idyllic offices to the ground. As our facility went up in cinders, so, too, seemingly, did all our jobs, all our ambitions, and all our dreams. The fire consumed everything—every file, every photograph, every piece of work in progress, every schedule, every telephone, pen, pencil, ruler, stamp, and paper clip. I do not exaggerate when I tell you that not even a corner of a memo survived. To compound the disaster, the press and many in our industry forecasted that our agency would be consumed as well, disappearing into the ether like so much smoke.

But by noon on the day that disaster struck, while the fire was still raging, our entire workforce had assembled back in a smaller property that had served as our offices just fifteen months earlier. These people didn't gather to mourn the bad luck that had stricken our company or update their résumés;

they arrived ready to go to work to rebuild their future. And rebuild it they did, with a ferocity that was inspiring.

The men and women of our account group scattered to clients' offices where they re-constructed our job histories by photocopying the comprehensive call reports we had used to confirm the events of each meeting. Our controller and treasurer commandeered our outside accountant's computer and loaded in the backup tape we had stored off-site in a safety deposit box, allowing the finance, media, and traffic groups to rebuild their work-in-process systems for every job in the agency. Our creative and production people scoured suppliers' files and re-created current ads from our engravers' raw films: whenever necessary, they also remade old ads from scratch. Forty-eight hours after the fire, Mullen was running flat out.

I am pleased to report that in the months following this disaster we didn't lose an account, we didn't lose an employee, and we didn't miss a single deadline. The only things we lost were a great deal of money and sleep. Even so, nine months later, by the end of 1987, the agency had not only grown by 20 percent, but had returned from its gross income (the money that sticks after all third party bills are paid) a 22.8 percent pretax profit.

If the stock market crash of October 19, 1987, was the starting gun that signaled the beginning of a recession, no one in our company heard it. In the late 1980s and early 1990s, Mullen continued to perform as if it were unaware of the national business contraction and unfazed by New England's heightened economic convulsions. Cumulative agency growth averaged 22 percent per year and pretax profits regularly topped 23 percent of gross income. Even in 1991, the worst year anyone can remember for the advertising business, our company grew by 13 percent and had operating profits of 21.4 percent, while much of our industry posted negative numbers of the same magnitude.

During the dismal six-year recession between 1987 and 1993, our employee workforce of between 50 and 155 people shared well over $10,000,000 in cash profits and earned nearly another $4,000,000 in distributed equity. What's particularly rewarding is that during the same period, we remained one of this country's agencies most honored for consistent creative excellence.

So, outsiders wondered, what was our secret? What mystical business formula did we have that caused this extraordinary renaissance? Well, I can tell you four factual reasons why our agency survived and prospered.

(1) *It wasn't our company's balance sheet that put the pieces back together after our 1987 fire, it was the sacrifices of employees who cared that our agency survived.* No one had to tell our managers what to do, and no one had to tell them that our needs were urgent. Their very jobs and personal lifestyles depended on our communal ability to rebuild each department, as did the jobs and lifestyles of all of their colleagues.

Carin Warner and her public relations staff made our managers available to the press on the theory that, if exposure was inevitable, we would be better off acting as heroic survivors than downtrodden victims. Our media and accounting groups, no longer bound by their primordial patched-together computing equipment and lumpy inter-department connections, took the opportunity to build a modern, borderless network and reorganize the entire way we integrated our business and financial data. Account people deepened their client relationships by facing fire-related issues squarely, then solving problems with a combination of energy, candor, and skill. They kept clients informed, truthfully, and diffused concerns with their unexpected confidence. In some cases, our brand teams even had the chance to offer new solutions to troubling old problems. More than one ad campaign was improved when pieced back together again.

Our maintenance crew installed lights, strung wire, cadged furniture from corporate neighbors, and rewove the physical fabric of our company at the same time the rest of their peers re-ignited its spirit. Everyone in the organization put in back-to-back-to-back ninety-hour weeks spurred by neither management requests nor the possibility of financial reward. These people weren't working like dogs to save *my* company; they were hustling to save *theirs*!

(2) *It wasn't new business legerdemain that doubled our company's size in the five years following that disaster; it was the energies of individuals whose careers benefited directly from that growth.* We always espoused the belief that the surest way to grow a job was to grow the company around it. But this practice works only if management is willing to recognize the developing skills of people already in place. In far too many growing companies, employees are often known as much for their foibles as they are for their skills, and that mixed reality is inevitably compared to a new hire's fabulous (albeit self-

sanitized) résumé. As a result, new people tend to make more money than those whose work made their job possible. At Mullen, we also hire people from the outside when a new set of specialized skills becomes important to our agency's talent mix, but we also take pains to value our existing employees and to give them the first chance at new opportunities. And if a new employee begins at a premium salary, our leveling process of restrained raises and smaller profit sharing rapidly moves it toward fairness.

Not too long ago my colleague and partner of two decades Paul Silverman was being ardently solicited for a job by a well-known out-of-work art director. "You people are beginning to attract major brand names," said the famous job-seeker, "and as you get involved with these bigger broadcast accounts, you're going to need someone like me."

"Just the opposite," replied Paul. "The people who created our future are going to get the opportunity to manage it. The people we're hiring now will be assigned to deal with our past."

(3) *If our profits remained strong, year after year, it was because of the motivation of people whose personal finances were directly improved by the company's financial success.* All deep

loyalties to me and our agency aside, the first obligation of every employee is to his own well-being and to that of his family. I have absolutely no doubt that each survivor of that horrendous 1987 fire went home the first night to coolly and methodically calculate the odds of our company's survival, and the odds of our prospering afterward. The fact that none of these perfectly rational, responsible professionals quit the next day spoke volumes about the value of linking each employee's financial success to that of the company.

(4) *The work that won us all those awards wasn't produced by a bunch of newly hired creative rock stars.* Year after year, our company is among a handful of those in the United States most consistently honored by the advertising industry. This doesn't happen because we raid other agencies for talent. It happens because we hire promising young people, teach them the values of our corporate culture, and give them the chance to do their best. Time and again, our greatest advertising has been created by home-grown employees. They didn't come to our company to build their personal portfolios, they came to build their careers.

Many people ask my advice on how to prepare a company for the kind of disaster that befell ours. I tell them all the same thing: build greatness into your organization at least five years before the calamity happens. (Since major problems rarely issue advance warnings, I'd suggest you start now.) A great company can survive and prosper in even the most mischievous of times only if the collective character of its employees is strong. That collective character won't be generated by a spreadsheet, nor will it serendipitously self-germinate. Character is developed in employees exactly as it is in children— through the examples of leaders who live and teach positive practices. As a manager, your number-one job is to foster the kind of character within your company that differentiates a great organization from one that is ordinary.

THEREFORE, this isn't a book about ethics and values, although both play an important role in the management practices I recommend. Rather, this is a hard-nosed formula for making money and being happy while doing so. In language and tone it is addressed to people who supervise others, whether the group numbers four, forty, four hundred, or four thousand. Still, it is my hope that these pragmatic philosophical practices will prove to be as useful to future supervisors as they are to those currently in power—particularly to young professionals who are intent on achieving or furthering a management career. And while business tips occasionally infiltrate the text, this is largely a book of concepts—simple but surgical philosophies with the power to unleash employee energies.

With luck, your organization will never have to endure as dramatic and calamitous an experience as our 1987 fire, but I promise you that, sooner or later, you and your people will be tested. In fact, the most insidious temptations often come masked as spectacular opportunities, usually financial.

In 1986, the public relations arm of our agency ran into a wonderful madman named Ken Meyers who was in the process of creating a new brand of popcorn that he called Smartfood. Now, when it comes to commodities, popcorn must be the ultimate example. To be sure, Ken's popcorn was coated with white cheddar cheese and tasted addictively delicious. But what differentiated Smartfood from all competitive snacks had nothing to do with the product:

1. Smartfood was sold in an iconoclastic black bag (a
   color traditionally anathema in food packaging).

2. Ken insisted Smartfood was *not* a popcorn. It was an *attitude*.

3. Under Ken's direction, *nothing* about the marketing of Smartfood followed conventional patterns.

For the first three years, our PR people organized lunatic guerrilla marketing promotions that built the consumption of Smartfood into a cult on college campuses, and the company went from $45,000 a year in sales to $15 million. Then the $6 billion Frito-Lay company purchased Smartfood in 1989 and decided to roll out its distribution nationally. For the first time in Mullen's history, our agency sensed a really big (over $10 million) advertising account on the horizon, but that dream reckoned without corporate America's bizarre sensibilities.

Just before we finally concluded a contract with Frito-Lay, we were named the agency for Veryfine, a fruit juice company that had made its mark in convenience stores by selling its product in individual ten-ounce resealable glass bottles. Traditionally, juice was something sold in a quart cardboard box that accompanied breakfast, but we saw that Veryfine's singles were being drunk by on-the-go young people all day long. So we asked ourselves and our client this question: "Why compete in the juice market when 80 percent of all the single-serving beverages in America are colas?" This considered, we recommended that Veryfine square off in the media as the healthful alternative to syrupy colas, and created a barrage of TV ads featuring young people, fast cuts, and hot music—very much in the quick-paced soft drink style. And since Pepsi Cola's brand position was more youthful and upbeat than Coke's, we portrayed Pepsi vending machines being ignored by young adults while they partied with the bright-colored juices from Veryfine.

Unfortunately, little Smartfood was owned by giant Frito-Lay—which in turn was owned by humongous Pepsi Cola. Even so, we saw no conflict of interest between these two clients, popcorn being a distant cousin to corn chips and not even liquid like a cola. Unburdened by any sense of competitive rivalry, we launched Smartfood nationally in late 1988 with a series of outrageous print ads and billboards, then repositioned Veryfine the following spring with our Pepsi-baiting TV commercials. When it became known at Frito-Lay that we were the culprits responsible for the Veryfine advertising, a call came in from their executive vice president demanding that we drop this attack "on Smartfood's mother brand."

"But all research shows that when you put a Veryfine vending machine next to a Pepsi machine, sales in both go *up*!" I pleaded.

"Probably true," said the executive VP, "but that argument is as useful to your case as throwing feathers at a charging elephant: Our CEO has Pepsi Cola running in his veins. How big is the Veryfine account anyway?"

"About $3 million," I replied.

"Well, we were $15 million over the last nine months, and next year's budget could be $25 million."

"But we can't fire a client who did nothing more than simply take our advice," I responded glumly. "Besides, our people would see this as a violation of the standards of our culture."

Still, the seduction continued. "Look, Jim, why don't you take a month or so to think about it. You know, we think you folks might be able to help us on other brands."

"Frankly, I'd love nothing better than another month of income from your account," I replied, "but it wouldn't be fair to you. I'm afraid I already know the answer. If Frito-Lay can't live with our Veryfine spots, then we'll have to resign the Smartfood account."

There was no heroism in this resignation, simply a clear

understanding of right and wrong backed up by a willingness to live by the culture that our senior management had preached and all of the people in our company embraced. The decision may have sacrificed an important account relationship, but it preserved our corporate integrity. Had I chosen the financially expedient path, I would have earned the disrespect of every person who had believed me every time I spoke about our company's values.

Providentially, Frito-Lay changed management six months later, and the new marketing director consolidated all its advertising relationships with a single New York agency. Sweeter still, by 1993 Veryfine had grown to become a $20 million account.

# 4

# GREATNESS AS A BUSINESS ART

AMONG THE MORE discouraging aspects of business life are the frequent encounters with companies whose philosophies and principles affirm the tradition that might equals right. Sad to say, America is peppered with organizations whose pursuit of success has contorted their operating structures into grim employee threshing machines, scything through souls, spirits, and (quite unknowingly) company profits with every slash of their bloodless financial rubrics. Ironically, these dehumanized and destructive supervisory practices often masquerade as leadership. The workaday philosophy of many large American corporations seems tò be *control* abetted by its henchman enforcer *fear*—not only a flawed way to do business, but a miserable way to live.

The destructive nature of this principle is revealed by the operating syllogism that defines common business practice: Title equals power, power equals leadership, therefore title equals leadership. In short, the boss may not always be right, but the boss is always the boss, and Big Daddy's uninformed judgments are to be questioned rarely and then only with exquisite delicacy. The control-minded manager's thoughtless comments must be tolerated without contradiction; without challenge, he is allowed to kill hundreds of hours of good work by people lower on the ladder of power; his whims demand priority over the work of his subordinates, even if their efforts are directed toward long-term organizational benefits; and his benevolence extends only the distance of his personal sight and hearing, and then only when it suits him to play Santa Claus. In cruel and fascinating emulation, managers reporting to the great boss will tend to mimic his indulgent actions, athletically exercising their own egos on the employees one level below. And so control and fear travel down through the system, and even out the doors to the company's associates and vendors.

This bureaucratic chain of principalities within kingdoms within empires is wrought in the name of efficiency and tied together with a cat's cradle of carefully delineated lines of command—at least on paper. In actual practice, this system of greater and lesser fiefdoms is massively inefficient. An idea from the bones of the organization must cross so many gate-keepers' moats on its journey to the top that few fresh inspirations survive the trip intact. Given the unfathomable web of responsibilities, personalities, and ambitions held by each mini-monarch along this chain, the criteria for the acceptance of any new concept are so profuse that few can meet them without massive compromise.

Anyone offering an original idea quickly finds herself in the "How Come" box. "How come we're wasting our advertising space giving people all these details?" one manager will ask. "People don't read that stuff anyway." Predictably, the next gatekeeper in the process will take an opposite position. "How come we aren't telling our customers everything there is to know about our product when we're the company that really has something to say?" Once in the How Come box, the innovator is on her own. The rule of meetings (Could it be that it's taught to all MBAs?) seems to be rigidly defined: In the face of top management disapproval, the most senior of the people who misdirected the process maintains silence, allowing the junior and more vulnerable to take the boss's hits. While I suppose that there is plenty of evidence around that this management system can lead to corporate bigness, it will never produce corporate greatness.

Bigness is easy to quantify and understand; greatness is quite a bit more elusive. Yet greatness truly is real and concrete. And as the saying goes about brilliance in art, we all know it when we see it.

I believe that a company has achieved greatness only when all the key groups who understand the organization best agree it has done so.

(1) *First and foremost, an organization's members must believe that they are working in a great environment.*

For a new employee, the true sense of any company's specialness doesn't arrive simultaneously with the first morning's cup of coffee. The standards of the company and its managers are absorbed osmotically over quite a long period of time— perhaps a year, perhaps more. As daily experiences flesh out each new employee's knowledge, they are examined in real time and then compared with what that person learned in life's previous business ventures or has gleaned from the stories of his peers.

By contrast, we in management delude ourselves that employees are motivated by the weighty thoughts proffered in our grand and gassy speeches, our broadsides of forceful policy mandates, and our streams of solicitously jolly memoranda on trivial subjects. What pitiful self-delusion! The fact is that, when managers address their organizations, they really are selling—and every one of their employees realizes it. The younger employees may cast down their eyes and retreat to private fantasies; older employees will appear dutifully enraptured and return all that false sincerity with a series of carefully timed nods and knowing glances—body language confirmations that add up to a flattering "You and I think alike, chief."

Accept these facts:

~ Your employees are smart. Otherwise, why did you hire them?

~ As a group, your employees see everything. *Everything!* Never do anything you aren't willing to see posted on the company bulletin board.

~ All employees talk about their jobs incessantly— with cohorts during office hours, with friends after work, with spouses at home. Every night millions of dinner table conversations begin with some version of, "Well, what did the old SOB say to you today?..." Certainly, what you tell your employees counts, but what you do in front of them counts a whole lot more.

In truth, employees don't learn nearly as much with their ears as they do with their eyes—by watching their managers' incidental actions and observing their private ways of operating. Duplicitous managers are like the emperor with invisible clothes. Because they think no one sees their furtive breaches of standards, they expect to be treated as virtuous—and often are by employees who want to get ahead. But many a manager's glass house would be shattered if he could listen in on the conversations around those same employees' dinner tables.

Not only is God in the details of daily business, so is greatness. When managers act with honesty and integrity, the cumulative mass of their everyday leadership creates business environments of fairness, loyalty, motivation, and employee happiness. Concordantly, they build microcultures that become the bulwarks of corporate strength, teaching each new employee the advantages of organizational greatness.

(2) *You must gain and maintain peer respect.*

The illusion of greatness is achieved much more cheaply than its reality. Your neighbors, children, and pets may be impressed by your clever sleights of simulated expertise, but your peers will not be so easily fooled. I learned this lesson from the august medical professor who was once my scientific mentor and has since become my friend.

In 1964, after I had taken a leave of absence from the Harvard Biophysics Lab to sail transatlantic and had become seduced by the lush wonders of life in the Caribbean, honor required me to declare my intentions personally to my superiors at the lab. So I dutifully returned home to finish off my experiments and gracefully orchestrate my departure from respectability. During my exit interview, the lab's imposing chief, Dr. Bert L. Vallee, listened thoughtfully to my youthful rationale for abandoning science in favor of (I hoped) tropical debauchery, and then related a story that gave me a whole new perspective on the meaning of true professionalism in any field:

"There was an old woman who lived, as she had for decades, over the little candy store from which she had eked out enough money to raise and educate her lawyer son. One day, the successful son returned home for a visit, resplendent in yachtsman's livery—blue blazer, red pants, cap with gold braided visor, and prestigious yacht club tie. 'Look, Ma,' he said, 'I bought a big boat and now I'm a captain.' 'Yes,' she replied, 'I can see by your clothes that you're a captain, but I have only one question. Among other captains are you a captain?'

"Jim," Bert Vallee said, "if you've decided to become a captain, be a real captain."

During my three years in the Caribbean I sailed the bottom off of that damned boat, and for fear of failing Bert Vallee's splendid standards I've sailed the bottom off of every job I've had ever since.

(3) A *leadership company must be both an artistic success and a commercial success in its customers' eyes.*

Customer respect has a great deal to do with your demonstrable results. While good PR and peer awards can be fun, other businesses will be more impressed by your solid financial strength. In many ways, leadership in profitability is as much a measure of corporate greatness as the most esteemed honor by the most revered industry authority.

To be blunt, you simply can't build a great company without making money, and lots of it. Besides, greatness is expensive. Better people cost more to employ because they do more and are willing to make more mistakes. Better people need better tools and require accelerated equipment expenditures. And better people deserve to know that their services are valued, and there's no denying money's ability to measure that.

But greatness in business is not an either/or proposition: you can have morality *and* profitability just as you can have ice cream *and* cake. Long before I had my first employee, the letterhead of Superfine Productions (precursor to Mullen Advertising) bore the whimsically elegant company motto, *Ars Gratia Pecunium*: Art for the Sake of Money. While this slogan no longer graces today's stationery, the concept has remained firmly among our corporate objectives for more than two decades.

(4) *You will be known in your industry by the companies you keep.*

Willingly or unwillingly, all companies are brands. Great brands, like birds, flock together.

I define a brand as nothing less (or more) than all of the thoughts, feelings, associations and expectations that any person experiences when she stumbles on a company's logo, its products, its headquarters, or any other integral symbol or design. In short, a company's brand is the surrogate for its corporate reputation, and as such is the best possible predictor of its future actions. A smart organization takes pains to define its brand identity and manage its public perceptions among all of its key constituencies by continuously reinforcing its core values. This isn't solely the responsibility of the advertising. Brands are built (or destroyed) by the cumulative impressions of every demonstration, seminar, trade exhibit, brochure, news event and promotion. Only a foolish organization will allow its brand perceptions to be shaped by the street or, worse yet, by its competitors.

In a sense, brands are very much like people. Take you, for instance: There are days when you are happy or sad, light-hearted or serious; there are occasions when you dress in your nine-piece business costume and others when it's blue jeans and T-shirt. Yet whatever your mood or involvement, there are some things you will *always* do and others that you will *never* do, and those who know you can predict both with high probability. The same is true for companies.

Therefore, just as you are known personally by your own interests and those of your friends, so, too, in the corporate world the businesses associated with you will partially define others' perceptions of your standards. Great brands tend to associate with, and beget, other great brands. Choose your corporate companions carefully.

WHAT MUST BE obvious to all by now is that for an organization to be recognized as great by jurors of this disparateness, some pretty wonderful things will have to occur. More troublesome yet, there is no silver-bullet way to make them happen easily or painlessly. It's just that the alternatives to a great company are so damned unappealing.

Near-miss organizations fall into one of two sad categories:

~ Those that settle for the pride of making great products but trudge along year after year with neither money nor growth. These companies rarely last very long: the fuel for creative passion is success and the fuel for success is enduring, profitable growth. As Eugene O'Neill said, "Contentment is a warm sty for the eaters and sleepers."

~ Those that create money and even business growth but offer no satisfaction to the workers involved. I have an old friend who is manager at a commercially successful agency, but one famous for its supple client compliance. As he puts it ruefully, "Ours is the company that bends over frontwards for its customers."

I believe firmly that you can have commercial success and, at the same time, experience the inestimable satisfaction of running an organization that achieves and maintains considerable respect. In fact, I believe that these qualities are inexorably linked.

While I've never worked in a very big company, it's my contention that a company's size should have (almost) nothing to do with its potential for greatness. What counts isn't mass, it's *attitude*. Regardless of the scope of the organization, the attitude that fosters greatness has to be rooted in the spirit of shared entrepreneurism. Entrepreneurship rewards the soul. It celebrates individuality and encourages the kinds of originality that vault over seemingly impossible barriers. Napoleon said that problems collapse as if so much architectural scaffolding before the power of a single word: faith.

In a smaller, growing business, senior managers spend their days nurturing ideas and people. In large organizations, they're driven to riding herd on process. But even a large organization can remain entrepreneurial if the spirit of entrepreneurship is nurtured in all its parts. Just as each cell in the human body functions both independently and cooperatively and this incredible cellular integration allows each of us to survive, a great company that is also a large company becomes the sum of its entrepreneurial work groups. In each group you'll find hands-on leaders involved with ideas and people, all connected by senior managers who understand and value the entrepreneurial process.

Ken Olsen, the founder of Digital Equipment Corporation, once told me a story about how he measured the value of his huge investment in research. "Research is terribly, terribly wasteful," Ken said. "We've got buildings full of brand-new pieces of equipment that people bought and never used. A designer gets an idea that needs some sort of new machine, so he runs off and orders the equipment, but by the time it comes, he's already on to something else. I've seen draftsmen walk into an engineering department with an armload of drawings for projects that were abandoned weeks earlier, and patternmakers deliver beautiful wood models that never even get unwrapped. Every year, someone comes to me and says, 'Ken, I can save Digital millions of dollars in research costs. We'll set up a timetable for each project and define a budget up front for the exact equipment needed. In three years, we'll deliver the project on time and be right on target with our costs. Absolutely nothing will be lost.' "

With that, Ken rested his big head on his cupped hand as he gazed into deep ceiling space, then added softly, "Except three years." (Currently, Digital may not be a great example of distributed entrepreneurship, but it started out that way. Pockets still flourished when we served DEC in the early nineties.)

So how does one begin to redefine an organization and direct it toward greatness? There's only one way—with a leadership leap of faith: absolute belief in the principles of employee capability and absolute trust that there's a soft land-ing at the end of the trip. However frightening it is for a leader to seize the initiative and actually *do something,* the reality is that the most dangerous course of action is inaction. You and your organization are far more secure if, as a manager, you are exercising an affirmative control on your circumstances rather than abandoning your destiny to the fates.

In this sense, I am reminded of a wonderful story about Tazio Nuvolari, a brilliant race car driver of the thirties and forties whose driving and logic both came right to the point. One day Nuvolari was having a rather frustrating conversation with a reporter who was trying to portray his profession as self-destructive lunacy.

"Aren't you afraid you will crash and be killed, Senor Nuvolari?" the reporter rudely demanded, incredulously expecting the Italian hero to break down and confess his mortal fear of vulnerability.

Nuvolari, no fool, countered her query with one of his own. "Tell me, madam, how do *you* expect to leave this world?"

The writer fumbled for a moment, then stated, "Why, I expect to die in bed."

Grasping her arm, Nuvolari gazed into her face with a look of solemn admiration. "What a brave woman you are," he said. "How do you have the courage to turn out the lights each night?"

# 5

## $\mathscr{T}$HE KICK-ASS WORKFORCE

IT IS VERY EASY for managers to confuse control with power. In actual practice, however, the more power a manager gives away the more power he accrues. Truly powerful managers will suppress their fear of losing control and find ways to turn employees loose, motivating them to achieve their best. If employees are correctly aimed and motivated, their collective ability to control their own destinies, catalyzed by their uninhibited ambition to excel, becomes management's greatest guarantor of organizational security. A dangerous, kick-ass workforce is part of the corporate culture of every great company I have ever known.

This is not exactly a new thought. In *The Way of Life*,

written about 565 B.C. by the Chinese philosopher Laotzu, there is a very wise poem:

A leader is best
When people barely know that he exists.
Not so good when people obey and acclaim him,
Worse when they despise him.
"Fail to honor people,
They fail to honor you";
But of a good leader, who talks little,
When his work is done, his aim fulfilled,
They will all say, "We did this ourselves."

Laotzu understood that managing is fundamentally the ability to motivate people. All successful manager/employee relationships are grounded by the principle of mutual professional respect. He also understood that there is no limit to how far you can go in life if you don't care who gets the credit.

I first engaged the wisdom of these concepts during my study of ethics at philosophy-driven Holy Cross College. Ever since, they have become the fundamental management precepts of my business life. From Ethics, I learned Aristotle's equation governing the immutable balance of human rights and responsibilities. For every right, Aristotle taught, there is a corresponding responsibility; and for every responsibility, there is a concordant right.

What an incredibly powerful thought! If you assign an employee the responsibility of carrying out a task, like it or not you have simultaneously assigned her all the rights that are necessary to achieve success. On the other hand, when she accepts all those delicious rights from you, she simultaneously shoulders the parallel burdens of the responsibility. By definition, rights and responsibilities are always in balance—even when we pretend they are not. If leaders don't have the courage and trust to give an employee the rights to do a job to the full measure of her capabilities, then it is management, not the employee, that bears the responsibility for the unsatisfactory work that very likely will follow.

Take a moment to gather your own observations on how rarely Aristotle's concept is exercised in typical American organizations. What a circus! Corporate leaders are forever demanding performance from middle managers who have little or no real power to hire, fire, spend, create, or schedule. At exactly the same time, misguided employees harass these same managers for higher budgets, more staff, additional perks, fancier titles, and bigger offices—all the while assuming a Teflon attitude toward the organization's real-world business problems. Management concerns itself with market competitiveness and annual profits: the workforce focuses on job security and employee benefits. Neither can take a more Olympian view without seeming to sell out to the enemy.

The net result is a stalemate. On one side, undeserving lower level scapegoats are sacrificed to management fire: on the other, employees greedily accept rights without embracing the corresponding responsibilities. So whose fault is it? Well, who's in control, the employee or the employer? Clearly, the ubiquitous business practice of delegating responsibility while centralizing rights is the beast that's eating our country's productivity. Yet it seems to me that the minute a manager is intellectually persuaded by Aristotle's equation of balanced responsibilities and rights, he is on his way to accepting the inevitability of a wonderfully dangerous workforce.

Embracing Aristotle's theory intellectually is, of course, a lot easier than putting it into action. The actual experience of ceding control is almost more than most of us can tolerate. At first, you feel helpless. Suddenly you find yourself an observer of the action rather than its field general, permitted just selected glimpses into the process because your enfranchised employees will be charging along paths they have divined without consulting wise old you. More often than not, the keyhole through which you are observing the action will reveal some rather alarming views.

"My God," your experienced managerial mind will exclaim, "that's *wrong!*" Every bit of traditional judgment you've been trained to exercise will seize your sensibilities and urge you to jump in and retake control, immediately! After all, isn't that what the company pays you to do?

No, it isn't. *The company expects you to help lead the entire organization toward success, not do every job all by yourself.* After all, even the most accomplished of us is just one person. If, as the best person in the group, your contribution carries the weight of, say, two good people, how incrementally valuable is that in an organization of forty or four hundred? My management philosophy is simple: If I disagree with one of our professionals who has thought about a problem for five weeks, and I've engaged it for just five minutes, the odds are overwhelming that she's right and I'm wrong. Therefore, since I attempt to be a thoroughly pragmatic person, I swallow my ego and go with the odds, accepting the responsible person's judgment over my own. This happens on a daily basis with our agency's creative products. I remind myself continually that I am not the target for most of our advertising. I'm white, affluent, and in my fifties—hardly a fair barometer for the aesthetic and cultural preferences of a younger, culturally diverse America.

Over time, leaders come to experience the reliability of their employees' thinking, and either gain confidence in their judgments or take steps to reduce both responsibilities and rights.

David Ogilvy, founder of a great advertising agency, wrote that his success rested on two fundamental principles: hiring smart people, then getting the hell out of their way. The former may be easier than the latter, since it's a lot more comfortable to assign people real responsibilities than it is to hand over real rights. Still, you must try. Blissful abandon isn't required, just a light management touch matched with a loose management cover. Stay interested and involved, but insist on independent decision-making. It will be instructive how often, as the complete process unfolds, you will appreciate the folly of your own partially informed judgments and the wisdom of your delegated champion's path.

In art school in the 1960s, a professor observed my frustration at repeated failures to capture on paper the soft grace of a life model with my blunt charcoal weapon. "Don't worry, Jim," he said. "The first hundred thousand drawings are the hardest. The second hundred thousand come a little easier." So, too, in management. After gaining some experience in the delegation of rights and responsibilities, you learn to trust your people and they learn that they are trusted. And when that happens, business magic follows.

What if, every now and then, it turns out that you were right and a normally reliable manager was wrong? Nothing, or at least nothing important. Shrug off your colleague's error with all the nonchalance you can muster. Mistakes happen all the time, but they only happen when things are moving along and getting done. Moreover, they happen equally often at every level in the company. The primary difference between senior management's bad judgments and junior management's occasional fumbles is that those of the upper echelon are far less visible and, often, far more serious. Think of it this way: If the company can survive the costly errors of its top managers, it will certainly survive the less expensive faux pas of its mid-level employees.

While it's important to be conscious of mistakes, it's more valuable to measure them by the right criteria. Your level of concern should relate less to the error's financial costs than to the reason the mistake occurred in the first place. Errors of judgment—mistakes made after thoughtful consideration by a caring professional—should be waved off with no comments except those of encouragement and support, regardless of the resulting costs. Mistakes traced to carelessness—those caused by the presumptions of someone too lazy to verify the facts—should be exposed and addressed vigorously, even when the financial damage is minor. No practice is more potentially damaging to a company than tolerance of the phrase "That's *probably* what the customer wanted." At the moment any employee abandons responsibility for a key decision, the difference between a large problem, a small problem, and no problem at all is purely in the hands of chance.

This was brought home to me early in my years as a race car driver when I excused myself from an error that, in graver circumstances, could have had mortal consequences for me and others. During practice for an amateur event, I spun a little Formula Ford, foolishly but harmlessly, a hundred yards or so away from other racing traffic. When I arrived back in the pits, my friend Skip Barber (head of a racing school and series bearing his name) was furious. "Hey, big deal, Skip," I said, "no one was even near me."

"*This* time!" he said.

He was right, of course. On another lap, I could have damaged my car, a friend, or maybe myself. The faster the cars I raced and the more competitive my racing became, the more I appreciated Skip's unassailable logic. And, in fact, we do apply the principle at our agency. An incorrect decision made by a production manager approving a printing job on a high-speed press can result in significant potential financial liabilities, but *no* decision could well cost us the confidence of our client as well as the entire account. History has shown that our write-offs from our production professionals' incorrect decisions are few and far between.

The delegation of rights and responsibilities is clearly an acquired taste but, like most of life's refined experiences, delicious when artfully practiced. Four years after founding our advertising agency, I had the good fortune to hire Paul Silverman, who was (and is) the smartest person I ever met. At that time, Paul was an unsuccessful novelist earning something less than a living as an editorial stringer to a mass merchandising trade journal. While his thinking and writing were first class, Paul's trade skills were a long way from those of a proficient advertising copywriter. Then art director Steve Haesche joined our company and began working with both Paul and me. While there's no question that Steve made my ads a whole lot better, it was even more evident that he was the nitro to Paul Silverman's glycerin.

A few years later, in 1981, our tiny band trooped to Boston to witness the awards show at which New England's advertising community honors its creative best. As a small, unknown shop among the giants, our agency didn't expect much recognition. The results not only shocked us, they electrified the entire community. Ads I had written won second-place silver bowls in seven of the most important consumer and trade categories, a triumphant sweep in anyone's book. Yet in every instance the first-place bowl was awarded to—Paul Silverman.

There was a message in that night for me. Soon afterward, I formalized Paul's position as our company's creative director and rapidly weaned myself from all creative involvement. It wasn't that I didn't enjoy the creative process or feel I could continue to be an effective copywriter; it was a matter of acknowledging that Paul was better, and that our most productive company course required space for Paul to grow without bumping into me. In 1992 Paul Silverman was recognized in a full-page ad by *The Wall Street Journal* as a Legend of Advertising, one of America's most honored and respected creative professionals. And for over twenty years he has remained my valued partner.

There is one more benefit to Aristotle's balance of rights and responsibilities that, ultimately, may constitute its most potent advantage. Matching obligation with authority gives employees the most motivating reward that a company can ever offer its people—the chance to do their very best, and to be happy.

Somehow, employee happiness is rarely a priority in management's agenda, but what could be more important? Happiness is as elemental an ingredient to business success as either intelligence or hard work! Consider Aristotle's definition of happiness (as interpreted by former Secretary of State Dean Acheson): "Happiness comes through the exercise of one's vital powers in a life that gives them scope."

Take a moment to think about what's being said:

~ *The exercise of one's vital powers:* When we do something important to us and do it as well as possible, we not only are likely to be successful, we're on our way to being happy.

~ *In a life that gives them scope:* As our skills, jobs, and careers expand, so, too, will our satisfaction.

In effect, Aristotle promises that if you work hard at things you believe in and you care about building their importance, you may not get to be rich and you may not get to be famous, but you're virtually guaranteed to live a happy life. Applied broadly, this principle makes it impossible not to conclude that the very same enfranchisement that makes a workforce kick-ass can also make its members happy.

The safest way to build a business is to create a dangerous workforce—motivated, enfranchised, and happy. Good people don't want to fail, they want to win. Happy people are energetic, attacking new problems with enthusiasm and shrugging off old problems with equanimity. Give people the right tools, the right objectives, and the right encouragement, and their thoughtfulness and innovation will astonish you.

In my experience, business is populated by very ordinary

people, even (especially?) at the highest levels. Yet it is extraordinary what ordinary people can accomplish if allowed to exercise their full capabilities.

Jeanne Ridgway began as my secretary when the agency employee population was exactly three. As our company grew, so did Jeanne's skills and performance, matching our organizational demands at each new level of size and complexity. Not long after she took over the management of the checkbook, Jeanne, who has always had a firm grasp on the theory of rights and responsibilities and who is one of the clearest-minded people I know, laid down the rules to me. "Mullen," she said, "you can mess with the checkbook only when you can prove to me that you can add and subtract more accurately than what I've seen so far."

I've never touched the checkbook since, and I've never regretted that decision. Today Jeanne is the treasurer of our corporation, responsible for the prudent management of hundreds of millions of dollars each year.

# 6

# $\mathscr{D}$ISCOVERING ENTREPRENEURISM—
# THE CATALYST OF GREATNESS

T H E R E  M A Y  B E a hundred college courses that purport to prepare a student to be an entrepreneurial business professional, but only one actively teaches the most important qualities of entrepreneurism. It isn't a business course at all, it's Philosophy. The study of philosophy requires the mind to grasp large, abstract concepts, then engage in a logical struggle toward a defensible judgment. Aristotle taught that if A equals B and B equals C, then A must equal C—the elemental theory behind all deductive reasoning. Whether this philosophical dialectic is learned in college or the school of hard knocks, its nonstop application creates the lifetime habit of straight-line thinking. In my book (and I suppose this is it!), entrepreneurism is nothing more than deductive reasoning applied with an indomitable will.

On a daily basis, you will hear managers support their business decisions by claiming some special sort of intuition. Baloney! Intuition is a genetic phenomenon that has everything to do with procreation and the protective response but has nothing to do with business reasoning. In fact, few things annoy me more than an assertion by colleague or client that "I know I'm right because I feel it in my gut." The gut is no substitute for the brain, and "gut feeling" is not only a silly business rationale, it's bad biology. Ever since prehistoric Og invented steak tartare, vertebrate intuition has been civilized down to a few of the body's most basic functions, and none of them relates to wise decision-making. Decisions don't come from "gut," they come from judgment, the prejudice that is formed when the brain parallel processes a few million experiential theses and antitheses, then refines this data into a simple "yes," "no," or "maybe." The earlier and more thoroughly the processing system is burned in, the faster and more certain the thought path toward capable judgments.

Why the emphasis on reasoned judgment? Because judgment is the only substantive intellectual attribute an entrepre-neur ever needs. Armed with judgment, one can acquire knowledge, all kinds and all amounts. I am living proof that given judgment and will, an entrepreneur can start a business unburdened by any substantive expertise whatsoever.

In the six months prior to starting my own agency, one of my responsibilities at Ted Hood's sail loft was creating the advertising—a duty that had been managed in-house previ-ously by a part-time yacht designer. Over the course of that period, I managed to generate a grand total of three ads by inventing a process so naive that it would horrify even the untutored interns who now pass through our company. First, I wrote the ad copy. Second (always at the last moment), I read the copy over the telephone to the publisher of *Yachting* magazine. That worthy gentleman, after debating the points of my ad (and often censoring what I thought were my best lines), wandered over to his file cabinet and selected a photo that he thought might work with the headline, then instructed his magazine staff to lay out the page. The first time Ted, I, or anyone saw the finished product was six weeks later, when the printed *Yachting* landed on our desks, trumpets blazing.

Armed with this truly laughable level of knowledge, I had the hubris to think I could start an advertising business. Very quickly the real world taught me that my skills were, at a minimum, ludicrously unprofessional, and that if I wanted to earn a living in this field, I really needed to learn the business. A smarter person might have appreciated the monumentality of this task, especially for an unvarnished communications amateur. Yet I approached my new business with eagerness because I was firmly in possession of two secret weapons: (1) I was willing to work like a dog, and (2) I was (and remain) the absolute master of the dumb question.

Dumb questions are rarely dumb. Early on, it became clear to me that by suppressing my ego and shamelessly admitting to ignorance, I could learn how to do anything. *Anything!* It turns out that the world is dying to be a teacher. Out there, everywhere, are zillions of people who are experts in the technical operations of every industry. Moreover, all these people are deeply proud of their expertise and nothing is more pleasing to them than the chance to display their knowledge. At the drop of a dumb question, most are eager to demonstrate their hard-won prowess to anyone who is genuinely, passionately interested—particularly those who might also become customers. Learning by dumb question takes humility, time, patience, persistence, respect, and concentration. But armed with these weapons, you can unravel the mysteries of the world.

The first day of my new career as a professional (ahem) advertising agent, I approached a printer named Tommy Noonan to do a flyer for my continuing patron, Ted Hood.

"Quantity?" Tom asked.

"A thousand," I said, "unless it's better to do two . . . or five . . . or ten."

"Stock?" Tom continued.

"Umm, what kinds are there?" I replied—which is a little like asking a painter to name all the possible color combinations that could be used to spiff up your bathroom.

Tom became tentative: "Number of halftones?" he asked with obvious suspicion.

"Well," I responded, "now we're moving into a technical area where I need your help."

"My God," Tommy gasped, "halftones are just photographs! I'll bet you don't even know the difference between letterpress and offset."

"True enough," I replied, "but if you teach me about how

this job should be done, you'll be well on your way to printing it for me."

And so Tommy did teach me the intricacies of printing and he did continue to print my brochures, for years and years. It is this skill in asking dumb questions, exercised over decades and combined with increasingly informed judgments, which has made me a marketing and advertising expert.

There was one other part of my background that gave direction to the entrepreneurial exercise, my experiences as a student and practitioner of science. In fact, it was the rigors of the scientific method that helped merge philosophy's deductive reasoning with a habit of systematic investigation. The disciplines I learned from science were to question and to quantify, two exercises that are absolutely vital for successful management.

My scientific mentor, Dr. Bert L. Vallee, built his distinguished career on the persistent and insistent use of the question "Why?" (plus, of course, endless work and not a little genius). Bert asked "Why?" until he got a real answer—not just a confident assertion. No matter how impressive a colleague's credentials or how authoritative the delivery of the theorem, if it didn't pass the Why Test, Bert didn't buy it.

In the lab's Monday morning meetings (seances that might have inspired Dorothy Parker's acerbic query, "What kind of fresh hell is this?"), Bert would grill each researcher with a persistent series of "Why?"'s until, inevitably, the associate would admit "I don't know." At this point, Bert would terminate the interrogation with a brisk "Find out," and go on to his next poor victim.

But Bert Vallee's dissection of his employees was kind compared to his scrutiny of his peers. Nothing stimulated Bert to apply the Why Test more than the uninformed pronouncements of a pretentious famous scientist. "All the time," he would say, "people are trying to pass off assertions as facts." Bert was persuaded only when the answer was demonstrable, quantifiably and repeatedly, and then he moved on.

It is for this reason that I discipline myself never to make an unquantified decision. Think of how many times you've listened to business associates eloquently elaborate some hypothetical idea—fleshing out its scope, illuminating its possibilities, and growing deeply excited by its splendid potential—when a minute or two of simple math would have revealed that the concept was financially tragically flawed. By the same token, think of the hours of wasted debate of the rightness or wrongness of some great principle when the crudest calculation would show that the financial consequences either way were trivial.

All concepts, intriguing and otherwise, must be evaluated in multiple ways, including their numerical implications. As often as not, bad numbers will sweep a seemingly brilliant idea into the dustbin of history, while encouraging one of apparently inconsequential importance to survive and thrive.

But, interestingly, of all of the weapons in my scientific quiver, the most useful has turned out to be one of the more arcane: Occam's Razor. In the early fourteenth century, William of Occam reasoned that "What can be accounted for by fewer assumptions is explained in vain by more." In short, whether the subject is math, marketing, or moon shots, the simplest solution is the one most likely to be correct. Complexity is to business decisions what cholesterol is to your body—little pockets of fat that clog up the arteries and so prevent the vital juices from building muscle. The most incisive minds are those that can arrive most quickly at the simplest, most elemental truths. There is such a thing as talent, and some leaders are just more gifted than others at selecting the right snowflake out of the blizzard. Yet we can all be more effective if we consciously work to keep things simple.

Earlier in this chapter I defined entrepreneurism as deductive reasoning applied with an indomitable will. It's also a drug so addictive that once exposed to it, few motivated managers will ever again be eager to live without its rush. Yet would that all entrepreneurship demanded were inquiry and determination. Unfortunately, there is another, less lovely quality that seems to be required of every true entrepreneur: the ability to endure adversity. While I cannot speak for entrepreneurs as a class, I am obliged to report to you that my own career is more memorable for its times of pain, fear, disappointment, and heartbreak than for its fleeting moments of glory. Not only must the entrepreneur never expect to fail, he must be the kind of person who has the ability to fail constantly without seeing failure as a pattern. For the entrepreneur to succeed over time, he must be able to absorb an endless series of knockdowns and, somehow, get back up with enough hope to take the next step forward.

I learned a lesson in this from watching Ted Turner during the late sixties when we were both deeply immersed in sailboat racing, and long before Ted was famous as a media mogul. Wherever Ted's life took him, he'd look for a sailboat race. No matter how provincial the regatta, Ted was willing to jump aboard any boat in the fleet—regardless of his lack of local knowledge, his experience with that particular kind of craft, or the length of the odds against him. When I asked Ted why a big-time international sailboat racer would risk the embarrassment of having some local kid clean his clock, he revealed something quite elemental in his character. "Oh, actually, Jim," he said, "I lose most of the time. For me, losing is just learning how to win."

The lessons Ted Turner learned from a thousand failures translated into a room full of silver that once included the America's Cup and, not incidentally, a multi-billion dollar communications empire.

# 7

## $\mathcal{I}$NSTITUTIONALIZING ENTREPRENEURSHIP

TWO CURIOUS THINGS happen to most entrepreneurs once the vital signs of their business begin to show some stability: First they centralize control, then they begin to graft onto their fragile entrepreneurship all the bureaucratic trappings of big business. Somehow the spirit that got the entrepreneurship going in the first place gets deep-sixed along the way. In most mature organizations, the entrepreneurial spirit is at best a part of the founder's legend, at worst a practice deemed obsolete by the new bureaucracy.

Yet within even the world's grayest, most turgid business structures, there are always natural entrepreneurs—people who devise ingenious ways to circumvent obstructive forms, procedures, and management just to get something done. Unfortunately, in traditional bureaucratic American corporations, the name by which these people are known usually isn't "entrepreneur," it's "troublemaker." I was one myself.

After a few seasons of the lush life of the Caribbean, I returned to New England to see my family and managed to land a job as captain of a small sailboat owned by a company that, among other things, manufactured yacht equipment. Somehow I had forgotten about the climatic vagaries of Massachusetts' seasons and when autumn rolled around, found myself reassigned to an indoor job, anchoring one of a phalanx of gray steel desks: five ranks across, fifty rows deep—the classic architectural office nightmare.

Since I knew a lot about yacht equipment and nothing about business, I was assigned to expedite the delivery of marine products and parts, a flow process as complicated as the wiring of an old house. I soon learned that deliveries of complicated assemblies like yacht winches could *never* be made quickly, because the system under which they were built conspired against success. By the time the company's daisy chain of bored, confused, and reluctant workers confronted the daunting requirements of the labyrinthine, multidepartmental paperwork, they were so discouraged that their ambition simply withered, resulting in delays and/or low quality products.

My method was simpler. First I got a list of the winches' components, walked out to the parts bins, and took them without authorization. Then I'd deliver the raw parts to the best machinist on the shop floor, a man who lived for the fun of doing something other than grinding out his days repetitively processing piecework. I'd tell him, "Charles, our boss [the yacht equipment company's president] needs these winches fast." Since the feckless bureaucratic president never went anywhere near the production line, I was pretty sure my white lie wouldn't get exposed.

While these winches were actually being built, I'd go back and tackle the tedious, time-wasting manufacturing forms, walking them through the building from engineering to parts-picking to inventory control and, finally, to shipping. Usually, if I really plugged along diligently, I could have all the paperwork finished just as the order was ready to be delivered. In those days, when the departmental phone rang, one of my colleagues habitually answered by saying, "Shipped it yesterday!" Customers laughed, but in the case of my winches, more often than not that statement was true.

This is the same company that, to fill in a box on its organizational grid, once offered me a promotion to advertising manager as long as I could live with one small hitch: The title and the raise were mine on the single condition that I *never speak* in a meeting with the agency! To me, the message was clear. The very last thing a good bureaucracy wants is a rogue thinker who is willing to fight for new ideas—which is why I didn't take the position offered and, shortly thereafter, removed myself from that stifling environment altogether.

Companies like this breed bureaucratic swamps that entrepreneurial leaders must work to drain. Those organizations that don't change are doomed to be overshadowed by others with vital entrepreneurial managements that value individual accomplishment. It's an incredible irony that the very business practices that nourish workers' souls are a manager's most powerful engines of profitability.

This isn't theory, it's fact. Entrepreneurism is the weapon that makes a dangerous workforce really powerful, and employee empowerment is a lot more than a slogan: It's the active component of every great company's culture. It's happened within our agency dozens of times—and not just at senior-management levels.

~ Laurie Miles, a young mechanical artist, realized that she had little chance to escape the production bullpen, so she taught herself computer graphics and then convinced me to invest in a serious and expensive system. Five years later, our entire creative group works exclusively on powerful graphics computers, with our pioneer Laurie a key manager in that department.

~ Ann Gohl, an out-of-work flight attendant, heard that we had a large, unused kitchen in the facility we had purchased a year earlier and pushed forward a series of proposals to institute an in-house lunch program. Each time I demurred, she came back with my objections answered and refinements that, ultimately, made the proposition irresistible. Ann ran our food service program for more than a year until the gentle schedule and strong benefits of flying lured her back to the skies. Today her successor, Liz Walkowicz, supervises a team of corporate chefs and operates one of the most popular and cost-effective departments in the agency.

~ Ian Hunter, our facilities manager, didn't get much satisfaction from just keeping our property clean and functional, so he kept pointing out the advantages of bringing additional jobs in-house—our painting, carpentry, mechanical maintenance, and even furniture making. When it first became necessary to add on to our agency's facility, Ian learned all he could from the outside professional contractors—so much that he no longer needs them. He now personally manages all our construction, even the major expansions of our building. Ian is also our first agency VP who started out in maintenance.

An organization's culture, after all, is nothing more than what the collective employee body believes and does. Therefore, it should be no surprise to any manager that her employees do what they're taught to do by their leaders, and what will get them ahead in their careers. If you teach employees bureaucracy, it will kill their spirit and, ultimately, your organization. If you teach employees entrepreneurism, it will not only make the workforce more effective, it will make your organization financially healthier, more efficient, and more fun for the management and managed alike.

In his master classes, Pablo Casals talked often of Bach and the incredible duality within his music. "Freedom with order," Casals called it, demonstrating the soaring emotion in Bach's unrestrained art while teaching his students to appreciate its underlying structure. Bach's music doesn't follow rules, it observes principles; but his genius was such that he played acrostics with notes at the same time he composed timeless musical invention. (I once read that in his *Christmas Oratario*, connecting certain chords on a key page forms the star of Bethlehem.) In business, freedom comes through institutionalized entrepreneurism, and order comes through an institutionalized understanding of the balance of rights with responsibilities.

The most useful way I know to infuse entrepreneurism into the fabric of an organization is for management to empower its employees absolutely, by climbing out on the limb of trust and then sawing it off. At Mullen, I go so far as to share with my colleagues an axiom that has given me the courage to make decisions in moments of doubt (and one which they then continually use against me): *It is always easier to get forgiveness than permission.*

In this all-too-human world, even the very best and most liberal manager can easily find risk in the word "yes," and substantial comfort in its counterpoint "no." In practice, we become adept at theatrically conditioning our yeses to come across as reasoned, thoughtful observations that, when all is said and done, actually translate into nos. We tactfully offer just enough latitude in our response so as to seem to be encouraging an employee's independent decision, but then we deliver that permission in a sufficiently negative tone to guarantee that the petitioner is prejudiced toward a course of zero action.

What kind of an outcome can be expected when a manager says to an employee, "Gosh, Ollie, you may be right, but if it were *my* decision—and of course it isn't—I'd sure want to think about the consequences a whole lot more before I ran off and committed a pile of company profits to the kind of thing you're talking about." In truth, the manager is saying no all along. Only a real fool of an employee wouldn't take that subliminal warning as a management directive to ditch that initiative and bail out fast.

It stands to reason, therefore, that in an entrepreneurial organization, where the balance between rights and responsibilities is well understood, the dumbest thing a productive person can do is discuss a responsible decision with senior management. "You idiot!" our brilliant and straightforward COO Joe Grimaldi once observed of a department head when the poor soul began volunteering details on a project about which I was unaware. "Why did you open your mouth and ask for Mullen's comments? This guy has an opinion on everything. Just what the hell are you going to say if the president doesn't agree with you?" Well, it's my fondest dream that the department head would have gone ahead and done what her best judgment dictated, but, in truth, that sure isn't the way the smart Chicago money would have bet.

An implied pressure is no less real than a management mandate, and Joe was absolutely correct. If our department head had thought about the decision carefully, was ready to accept full responsibility for its outcome, and didn't want to hear a no, she was better off not soliciting my opinion.

Management does have a constructive role to play in departmental decision-making, however. In fact, managers are paid their hefty salaries on the assumption that they are capable of offering sage counsel to their junior colleagues, to serve as their compassionate mentors and to provide both encouragement for their actions and protection against their doubters. But it's a lot to expect that a struggling-but-proud employee will seek out his manager and actually ask for help. After all, responsible employees are trying to demonstrate competence and confidence, not indecision and uncertainty. Better managers will actually dig for the problems where they occur, out there in the work areas of people who are creating the products.

A manager's office is a scary place. Even trusting employees enter superiors' domains only when they have a very specific (and usually positive) agenda. Get out of your work spaces and into theirs. Walk in, admire whatever project is on the desk, and say, "Hey, what's going on?" Simplistic as that sounds, it works. Employees automatically will relate your indiscriminate question to whatever is bothering them most at the moment, and utilize this serendipitous conversation to get their problem solved. Not only will they tell you what is going on, but often the news will shock the hell out of you. If Roger Smith had spent half his time in the 1970s and 1980s marching into the offices of the GM employees who were dutifully creating Detroit's plastic pachyderms and asked, "What's going on?" I guarantee you that the Japanese-built Lexus and Infiniti wouldn't exist today.

"What's going on?" is a big time, open-ended question that invites candid responses. Believe me, your employees know the answer to that question and how to fix the problems it will uncover. You just need to get the process rolling. "What's going on?" isn't a casual inquiry; it's the entrepreneurial manager's most effective weapon.

Usually, as the employee unburdens himself to you, he will tend to do so with specific references to specific issues, tempting wise old you to leap in with the managerial tweaks and adjustments that will get the problem solved and the process moving again. Given your genius, the desired effect may actually occur and all associated will feel jolly about the sudden improvement in results. But what's actually happened is that both the employee and the company got shortchanged. The *process* was not improved, nor were the capabilities of the responsible employee expanded. The next time a problem appears on that person's desk, you might not wander by at the propitious moment, and the employee's decisions will remain duller than they could have been if you had been a more effective manager.

The best way to move the company ahead isn't for managers to inject themselves into the center of the decision-making process, but to use each opportunity to hone the decision-making skills of the front-line troops. Don't teach facts, teach entrepreneurism. Don't give solutions, illuminate the possibilities. Don't solve problems, teach problem-solving. Picasso showed great insight when he observed that "computers are useless: They can only give you answers."

Rather than directing the outcome of the process, use your superior experience to help segment and position the problem so that the employee can attack it in nice, logical, manageable bites. If he can merge the experience gained through your problem-solving process with the knowledge he already has from his own superior operational involvement, the solutions effected are very likely to be terrific— today, tomorrow, and forever. More important, you have added one more entrepreneurial warrior to your growing dangerous workforce.

Not only will your habit of building entrepreneurism

help your employees get ahead, but their improved efforts will do wonders for your own career. In the early 1980s, I was codriving a turbo-charged Porsche 935 with a spirited Californian who was both a hot driver and a good mechanic. Pulling into the pits during a practice session, he'd say to the crew, "Crank some more weight onto the outside rear tire, raise the lip on the spoiler a quarter of an inch, and soften the rear sway bar." It was impressive. This was a driver who could actually analyze the problem of the car's adhesion to the road at multiple points on the track, then form solutions in his mind—all while he was still out on the race course. Unmechanical me, barely able to distinguish among the three pedals on the race car's floor, was totally unprepared to match my codriver's expertise. By contrast, I'd concentrate hard on understanding what was happening to the car at every point on the course, then simply report those circumstances in detail to the crew chief and mechanics. "The rear of the car is getting loose in the fast sweeper, but I can't get the front to stick in the hairpin turn. How can we get more power down in both places?"

Because my codriver was mechanically knowledgeable, he instructed the crew on how to fix the car. Because I recognized the separation between my job and that of the mechanics, I simply defined and narrowed the problem and counted on the entrepreneurial crew to apply their thoughtful collective expertise to make the correct adjustments.

In the succeeding years, after my friend and I went our separate ways, we both moved up to major teams that ran the faster and infinitely more complex GT prototype race cars. Because prototypes covered more ground more quickly, they required a greater mental commitment and more subtle technique, and the differences in our driving habits began to show. At 200 mph (a football field every second), my former teammate was too busy to drive with total concentration and still figure out the Rubic's cube of chassis adjustments. I just got in and drove, experiencing what happened at each point on the track and transmitting that information as clearly as possible to the crew. Ultimately, it was the combined problem-solving skills of our whole team—driver, crew chief, and mechanics—that put a car on the track that was inherently faster.

The soundest advice I ever got in racing was this: If you want to win, drive a fast car. I figured out pretty early in the game that, since every track is different, the surest way to

have a fast car is to have a skilled, entrepreneurially motivated crew preparing it. I was never as talented a driver as
many others on the IMSA circuit, but over the years I won a
lot of races.

# 8

## *C*AN CREATIVE PEOPLE
## BE MANAGED?

THERE'S A CLICHÉ among account service people in
our industry that goes "Advertising would be a great business
if it weren't for the creative types." This couldn't be more
ridiculous. There wouldn't be an advertising business without
the creative types, nor would the account service people have
anything to sell. Considered globally, there wouldn't be many
things in this world that would be worth owning or doing if it
weren't for the imagination, inventiveness, wonder and magic
of the men and women who infuse our myriad goods and services with their spirit-raising creativity.

In every industry, no person is more prized than the artist,
be she a chef, a diva, an airframe designer, a computer pro-

grammer, or a deal maker. On the other hand, no person is more mercurial, less reasonable, or quicker to be insensitive and even abusive to colleagues, managers, and customers alike. No wonder they are often described as "unmanageable."

To make managing creative people even more difficult, most are quite articulate in their contrariness. Yet because they tend to be nonlinear thinkers, the deductiveness of their reasoning is consistently short-circuited by dazzling leaps of imagination and inventive excursions around points of logic. Moreover, they always approach a discussion from exactly the same perspective—their own. Creative people begin a dialogue with bountiful quantities of their own sympathy and end it unshakably certain of their unique point of view.

In fact, creative people are (and I write this in the kindest and most admiring way) very much like children—people you love who fill you with delight one moment, then twist you into apoplexy the next. They don't (usually) mean to frustrate you. It's just that, in the world of the truly creative, they are always at the center, and they find it genuinely impossible to understand why everyone else doesn't see life through their eyes.

Every industry has its creative factions, and every industry deals with them the same way: We spoil them. Advertising pampers its art directors and copywriters, a restaurant indulges its chefs, computer manufacturers coddle their software writers, and clothing manufacturers handle designers with velvet gloves. There are any number of reasons we do so: because they delight us, of course, but also because we fear them and because we've learned that we can't live without them. Yet the ultimate business reason we indulge, coddle, pamper, and spoil our creative colleagues is—blasphemy of blasphemies—because they deserve it.

Creative people, like the rich, really are different—neither good nor bad, productive nor unproductive, frugal nor wasteful—just different. Yet if you as a manager can get a handle on how to motivate creative people, they will be among the most caring and hardest working people in your company.

What is often overlooked by managers and co-workers when they criticize creative people is that the world only prizes those who actually produce great things. Frauds and second-rate creative talents are universally scorned, mocked, and vilified with energetic cruelty. It's rare that an audience will boo a boring academic lecturer, but just let an actor blow a line or a musician fluff a note, and the crowd will exercise its opinion with swift and noisy justice.

In his preface to *The Doctor's Dilemma*, George Bernard Shaw wrote this brilliantly incisive description of the creative temperament:

". . . The common man may have to found his self-respect on sobriety, honesty and industry; but . . . an artist needs no such props for his sense of dignity. . . . An actor, a painter, a composer, an author, may be as selfish as he likes without reproach from the public if only his art is superb; and he cannot fulfill this condition without sufficient effort and sacrifice to make him feel noble and martyred in spite of his selfishness."

Shaw also observed the simple truth that "hardly any of us has the ethical energy for more than one really inflexible point of honor." The inflexible point of honor for creative people is always their work. In pursuit of their art they are willing to sacrifice their time, energy, and health—and, not incidentally, yours as well.

Can, therefore, creatives be managed? Of course, but not in conventional management terms. I believe that creative employees respond to motivation more directly and energetically than any other class of professionals, but what energizes them best is the unfettered chance to exercise their creative powers. Therefore, your job (as well as your sole option) is to align the company's goals with theirs, and not vice versa. Give them the praise they crave, create opportunities for their public recognition (such as awards shows), and honor them in front of their peers. Only when you truly understand the creative person's motivations can you, jujitsu-like, use that irresistible momentum to achieve the broader organizational objectives.

Begin by accepting the creative temperament, and by understanding its sometimes delightful, sometimes damaging dynamics. Then organize for success: Fit the right creative person to the right job from the beginning, or bear the unpleasant consequences. Don't ask a senior talent to take on a problem unless you are willing to live with a strong, and perhaps unconventional, solution. Then, once the idea meets the strategic objectives, don't expect much malleability in the way it's expressed. Asking strong creative people for change or compromise is largely futile. Sure, they'll accept a little peripheral alteration here or there, but they'll protect the core of their concepts like mother bulldogs. Their seeming insensitivity to your "practical" needs has nothing to do with a lack of discipline or an inability to understand what you are asking. It has everything to do with their own self-esteem. And creative people's self-esteem is exclusively a function of their need to reach out to the new, the different, the unusual, and the astonishing.

In my experience, creative people approach most new assignments with optimism and excitement. They are quietly certain that they, perhaps uniquely, can solve the problem at hand and do so in a way that will draw the breathless admiration of peers and strangers alike. In fact, most creative failures stem directly from bad management, usually originating in a poorly thought out or incomplete definition of the problem at hand.

For creative professionals in the advertising business, nothing is more stimulating or fun than a new business pitch. Why? Because *communally* the research, marketing, and creative groups within the agency will identify the prospective client's opportunities and define a *clear, logical strategy to achieve them.* This strategy may or may not be precisely accurate in the real world since it is based on limited experience and little or no client involvement. It does, however, by virtue of its informational innocence, have some singular creative advantages: It is unencumbered by dubious client taste or judgment, and it doesn't waver in direction after the work is under way.

It is my experience that creative people become recalcitrant and uncooperative only when they have struggled and sacrificed to develop a truly inventive answer to a problem only to find that, *post facto*, the question has changed. The strongest assistance you can give your creative colleagues is to point them in the right direction from the beginning. Before you even involve them, make sure that you have already defined the job by a clear (written) statement of the strategic objectives and a well-considered set of priorities. Then stand back and let your creative associates exercise their taste and art. Use your powers of logic to judge the accuracy, the relevance, and the clarity of their product, but allow your trusted creative colleagues free rein in deciding the emotional qualities of the expression.

I believe that the safest way to work successfully with creative people is to maintain an ongoing involvement, with significant attention to the process at the beginning and the end but with minimal interference during the middle parts. Begin by clearly and thoughtfully defining the problem, then carefully reviewing their earliest, roughest attempts at solutions. This allows you to verify the continuing health of the strategic objective and to give honest reactions to the paths they are proposing to take. Even so, never, *never* insist that an idea you initially dislike be dropped. I can't tell you how many times I've looked at a copywriter's ideas for an ad and mentally rejected headlines as too literal, or too loose, or simply uninspired. Yet I found that when these same words were matched with an unexpected photo or graphic design, an idea took flight that transcended the sum of its individual components. Some of the greatest campaigns our company has produced began as ideas I hated.

In the blizzard year of 1978, our fledgling agency undertook its first and last political campaign—George Atkins for Selectman in Salem, Massachusetts. True to their insightful understanding of what really counts in small towns, Paul Silverman and Steve Haesche proposed a campaign with visuals that showed blunt head-and-shoulders photos of George under powerful headlines like "This face can move a snowplow." Since I didn't have the courage to take work this strong to a conservative client, I found a dozen ways to drive the advertising campaign back to boring restatements of highbrow political strategies. The results were brutal. In the history of local politics, it's doubtful that anyone ever got poorer returns than George Atkins. As he himself ruefully observed, "Either my wife or my mother must not have voted for me."

As you visit creative work in progress, always be encouraging, even when the initial ideas have strayed from the agreed-upon strategic objectives. Creative people feed on approval, and it's important to find *something* good about even the weakest effort before you gently nudge the work back toward the strategy. Be prepared to spend time listening (probably several times) to the reasons why they chose the direction they did. In all likelihood, you'll find a point within that explanation that represents the seed of the correct solution. Grasp it and play it back to your creative colleagues with positiveness and enthusiasm, using it as a wedge to set the concept back on track. Remember also that creative people's perspectives must be treated as valuable, even when off base. Otherwise, you are likely to inflict some bruises on fragile egos.

When you must reject an idea, do your best to phrase your demurral in terms that permit soft emotional landings. Repeated insensitive dismissals are likely to foster the habit of acquiescence in the weaker creative souls and truculence in the strong. Either way, your organization has reduced the potential contribution of several of its strongest assets.

Once the creative product is produced, that's the time to assert your management power by supporting the creative effort with the same passion and energy as those who developed it. It is so easy, and so destructive, for management to sell a creative product down the river when faced with strenuous client objections. It isn't just the weeks of labor that are being abandoned, it's a piece of your creative colleague's heart. Worse yet, the solution that you are allowing the client to wave away may not just be the *best* answer to the problem, it may be the *only* answer. New ideas are fragile, and your creative partners deserve your commitment to fight for their integrity. Win or lose, this united front will bond you as a team and encourage your creative associates to trust your judgment and believe in your support for future projects.

Not all great creative people are great creative leaders, but all great creative leaders are, themselves, deeply competent at their crafts. Moreover, great creative leaders are able to understand the broader implications of their work, and that of others, for the larger aspects of business itself. Not only are they able to judge the creative effectiveness of the art, but also they can visualize its influence on short- and long-term strategies. Our chief creative officer, Paul Silverman, and his co-creative director, Edward Boches, are as different as two people can be with management styles as individual as their thinking and writing. Yet because they share the same standards of intelligence and care, both motivate our creative department toward the single objective of greatness by offering at least a couple of paths toward that end.

Strong creative leaders such as Paul, Edward, and the wild bunch they lead are never easy to live with, but the wonderful spirit they bring to our products is worth the disorder they wreak upon our lives. Bill Bernbach, advertising's universally esteemed saint, spoke as persuasively about the creative process as he did about the virtues of the early Volkswagens. His observations were about advertising, but they apply to every creative activity in the world.

The true instrument of discovery is not logic, it's taste.

Analyzing creative work is like dissecting a frog. It's an unpleasant and destructive business, especially for the frog.

An appeal to logic never works. The brain is not an instrument of logic at all. It's an organ of survival, like fangs or claws. So the brain doesn't search for truth, it searches for advantage.

The irony is that the most gossamer things, the most indefinable things, so delicate that they are dissipated by analysis, turn out to be the things that create those big, beautiful numbers in your profit statement.

Not only can creative people be managed well, they can be managed without exploiting their sensitivity, so that the artists become and remain well regarded by their fellow employees and by themselves. The management of your creative employees may be one of your greatest challenges, but I promise you that your successful efforts will provide your greatest rewards.

# 9

## HIRING A KICK-ASS WORKFORCE

WHEN *THE LONDON TIMES* was tossed to the curb one misty dawn in 1900, it carried the best ad that has ever been written. The copy was short and plain; there were no photos or illustrations; and the placement was terrible, stuffed as it was among a jumble of similar ads in the newspaper's cluttered classified section. Yet this ad changed the world.

> Men wanted for a hazardous journey. Small wages, bitter cold, long months of complete darkness, constant danger, safe return doubtful. Honor and recognition in case of success.
>
> Ernest Shackleton

By the time Shackleton opened the doors to the office for his South Pole expedition, there was a line of applicants that wound twice around the city block.

Shackleton understood something that every good military and civilian leader has learned through experience: Good people aren't afraid of trying something difficult, even if it's dangerous. Rather, they're much more afraid of living their lives in oppressive boredom.

Hiring wisely may be the most challenging of all managerial skills, but if you believe in the concepts of teamwork and delegated responsibilities, it is one of your most critical jobs. I've developed a handful of criteria that, while no guarantee of success, increase the odds of success from random chance to high probability.

(1) *Hire people who are smart.* The one thing you can't teach, the one problem you can't fix, the one habit you can't adjust is native intelligence. It stands to reason that, all other things being equal, the more robust their thinking power the better (faster, deeper, sharper) the solutions that person can bring to every problem.

A truly terrible client once said one good thing to me: "Your senior hires are the most important, because A-level people will then hire other A-level people, but B's will hire C's, who'll hire D's. . . ." The first moral of this tale is the inherent wisdom of the advice. The second is that you can learn from anyone, even a person whose general performance is small endorsement of his abilities.

(2) *Hire people who are simplifiers.* Of all the infinitely possible ways to segment the world, the most useful for building a business is the practice of sorting out potential job candidates into the categories of simplifiers and complexifiers. Simplifiers have an innate appreciation for Occam's Razor and will strip away distractions until they get to the nubbin of a situation, no matter how embarrassingly obvious the solution then appears. Complexifiers habitually become bundled up in their own underwear by assigning as much importance and time to every superficial anomaly, exception, and contradiction as to the main point itself. The net effect of a complexifier's involvement in any project is more work, long delivery delays, and an inexorable dilution of quality. Moreover, there is no one better at putting good people in the "How Come" box than a complexifier.

Beware of potential hires who have been trained in organizations with elaborate processes.

(3) *Hire people who really are willing to commit themselves.* Commitment has nothing to do with robotic diligence, martyrish submersion into hard work, or maniacal attention to detail. Commitment has to do with an inherent sense of personal satisfaction that comes from a job well done, independent of the potential for tangible reward or the world's accolades. The greatest self-delusion in business is that of the employee who says, "The reason I didn't do a great job on this assignment is because the project was *boring.* Now, if you only gave me something interesting to do, then I'd show you what a terrific performer I can be." This is the chronic slacker's snare and delusion. Truly valuable people have too much pride to apply average standards even to the most menial task. By doing every little job well, committed people make themselves so valuable that their managers can't wait to pile on ever-increasing amounts of responsibility and, of course, reward.

Now, in an interviewing situation, every prospect will *say* that he's committed. Remember Mullen's Interviewing Axiom: Don't listen with your ears, listen with your eyes. Look at what the people's résumés really say: Have they ever committed themselves—not just in a job, but in a sport, a band, a church group, someplace—really and truly committed themselves deeply, with sacrifice and passion?

When I use the word "committed" I apply the standards of the late Bill France, organizer of NASCAR, which promotes America's greatest racing event, the Grand National stock car championship. Back in the 1950s, when NASCAR was less a true series than a ragged sequence of races, it had a few grand spectacles and many more struggling rural venues. The major teams cherry-picked their events, entering the high-dollar popular races and passing on the smaller tracks whose purses were weak. But Bill France knew that the real money would come only when the public imagination could be focused, by a series championship, on one overall winner, and that meant that all the teams had to enter all the races.

Junior Johnson, NASCAR's top driver and subject of Tom Wolfe's colorful biography *The Last American Hero*, was one of those major box office draws who habitually skipped the smaller races. One morning over breakfast, France collared Johnson and told him that, to make the NASCAR series really work, Junior would have to become more committed. Junior protested that he was already committed; Bill said he wasn't. "You're involved, Junior," Bill said, "but you're not committed," a statement that confused Junior so much that he asked Bill to explain the difference.

"Well, Junior," Bill replied, "in the production of that splendid plate of bacon and eggs you just ate, I think we'd agree that, while the hen was *involved*, only the pig was *committed!*"

(4) *Hire people who are different*. You already have your own unique points of view, and they are already available to the company nonstop. Why in the world would you want to pay someone merely to echo the same thoughts? I have always looked for people who share my objectives and values, but who have a natural disposition toward perspectives I am unlikely to originate, or even accept without argument. When I hear comments like "weird" and "she's not like us" about a qualified candidate for an open job, I break into inward smiles: We've found our new employee.

My two most senior colleagues are Paul Silverman, our chief creative officer, and Joe Grimaldi, our chief operating officer. Rarely do the three of us agree on anything, but usually there are just two, not three, divergent points of view—a majority and a minority. Inevitably, the minority opinion holder will accede to the majority pair with grace, confident in the odds that his two smart, caring, and respected colleagues are twice as likely to be right as wrong. It's not a matter of votes (we never vote), it's a matter of logic, and intellectual honesty. I know: I'm often odd man out.

(5) *Hire people who show signs of entrepreneurship.* You need to institutionalize entrepreneurship, but you can't do it with people who are born bureaucrats. Look for signs of independence, even trouble-making, in your interviewee's history. In an entrepreneurial organization, a major portion of every person's job is inventing her future by thinking about the ways evolving business challenges will affect her responsibilities. Remember that no one has a better grasp of the operational realities of any job than the individual who's doing it. Therefore, no one is in a better position to make the progress more effective and, since the person is an emerging entrepreneur, no one has more motivation to do so.

My friend and one-time codriver Bob Akin once owned a race car designed in a way that proved to be inherently flawed. Rather than ditch this expensive piece of machinery and impoverish the race team by building a new car, entrepreneurial Bob began isolating the problems one by one and minimizing them. When another driver commented sarcastically on the process, Bob replied, "Well, maybe I can't make a race horse out of a pig—but I can make an awfully fast pig."

(6) *Listen, really listen, to what candidates tell you.* I was warned against many of my most egregious hiring mistakes by the candidates themselves. One was a big, warm, experienced direct marketer who pulled from his business suit a glittering résumé with account management experience at all the right places. "But I'm really not a very good account manager," he said a number of times, "I'm really a creative person."

"Naah," I replied, "look at your background! You're the perfect person to run our direct marketing division." After I tempted him with a sizable salary and a seductive package of perks, the truth emerged. My new department head, it turns out, couldn't manage anything more complicated than a hearty lunch. Yet, true to his word, he was an unending source of brilliant, innovative ideas—none of which our company had the account staff to execute. He was exactly what he said—a creative person. I didn't listen to him. We both suffered.

* * *

SINCE IT IS IMPOSSIBLE to evaluate a job candidate perfectly, the likelihood of error is huge, even for the most diligent interviewer. It's also true that people who have been mediocre in one company's environment can be fabulous in another. Therefore, the only real way to find out if the fit is correct and the candidate has the makings of an entrepreneur is to take a deep breath, make the hire, and see what happens. That said, recognize also that future success or failure will be fundamentally influenced by what you do as the new employee settles in to the job. May I suggest six critical practices for you to pursue?

(1) *Assign someone to teach each new person the ropes, including the company culture.* I know, I know, I've already said that the company culture is learned osmotically from a myriad of observed examples of organizational philosophies in action. Still, by asking an old hand to spend time training the new person in operational procedures, you'll find that the two will inevitably end up discussing why things are done or not done in certain ways, and some of the reasons will be cultural. It's not that the trainee will unquestioningly accept his mentor's endorsement of the company's cultural idiosyncrasies, but he

will at least be given hooks onto which he can hang future observations.

If there is an operational flaw common to many entrepreneurial companies, it's that they undervalue job training for new people. Poor or no training may be OK when the organization is smaller, but larger groups need some combination of a peer buddy system and direct management instruction. Good people want to do what you want them to do. Just don't forget to tell them!

(2) *Watch, don't ask.* Every new employee will tell you that his world is completely rosyola, regardless of how stupid he feels his opening assignments are. What else would you expect—that he'd tell his manager how much he hates his new job? Therefore, it pays to listen with your eyes, watching for signals that warn of increasing discomfort or growing frustration. When you see either, get involved.

Amy Watt joined our agency as a mechanical artist, a person who (before the era of computer graphics) physically pasted type and photostats onto white boards, preparing the correctly formatted ads for shipment to an engraver. While mechanical artists are not the primary designers of ads, they do apply a great deal of visual judgment in their work and require a high level of manual dexterity to move ads along quickly. Amy was both slow and awkward.

One day our creative director, Paul Silverman, came to me and said, "I'm going to do something about Amy, Jim, but not what you'd think. I'm going to make her an assistant art director." I was floored. Here was someone failing at a production job, and Paul had decided to give her a promotion! "What I've noticed," said Paul, "is that she's not very good with her hands but she's terrific with her brain." Amy's now our associate creative director and co-originator of a raft of award-winning work, including the legendary Smartfoods campaign.

(3) *The strength/weakness syndrome.* I've noticed that as soon as I've found what an employee does best, I have concurrently located his main vulnerability. If an employee is careful, accurate, and reliable, he's equally likely to be slow and able to focus on jobs only sequentially. If another employee can keep a dozen balls spinning in the air simultaneously, odds are pretty good his appreciation for the nuances of each of these will be minimal. The mirror image of every person's strength is his weakness. Therefore, as you are applauding an employee's

success at a task well handled, remind yourself to match that person with someone of a complementary character in a situation where the opposite skills will be required.

(4) *Mash not square pegs into round holes.* It is far less frustrating and more productive to refine a job description to suit its occupant's nature than to get a willful adult to change her lifelong habits. I mean, if her mother couldn't correct her before the age of five, what chance do you have now that she has had a few decades of practice? As Brer Rabbit once said in a song, "Accentuate the positive and eliminate the negative" by orienting the job's important obligations toward your employee's strengths. If you have a creative genius in your company who can't keep a schedule or fill out paperwork, save your critical breath and assign the brilliant one a nanny—an administrative assistant with a mania for organization, neatness, and detail. Both people will be happy, and together they'll elevate their mutual productivity to levels that trivialize any associated incremental costs.

(5) *Muzzle management's guns.* Unfortunately, the world has been taught inordinate respect for titles, because all our lives we've associated titles with power. Think how even we

Americans, the ultimate practitioners of democracy, go all atwitter when we meet some European with a threadbare, hand-me-down vestige of royalty. More or less the same thing happens in industry. Since most of your employees will have had some job experience before arriving on your doorstep, expect a strong measure of undeserved deference in the early stages of your relationship. Very likely, that demeanor was required in the places they used to work. Don't abuse this temporary obeisance by inflating your persona to match your new employees' perceptions. You haven't yet won respect, and your power will be all the more secure if it's used only in times of urgent need.

My immediate superior at the Harvard Biophysics Lab was Dr. Chuzo Ida, a bright, happy, unprepossessing wisp of a man, modest beyond all measure. Quite by accident, one of his Japanese colleagues let slip the fact that Chuzo was an expert in oriental martial arts. At twenty-two, I found the idea of macho invulnerability a thrilling concept.

"Chuzo," I asked, anticipating some delicious Clint Eastwood–type stories, "what do you do when someone starts pushing you around?"

"Why, Jim," Chuzo said firmly, "I run!"

"Run?" I muttered with palpable disappointment. "You mean you run away?"

"Yes," said Chuzo, "I run—but I run with *confidence!*"

# 10

## *L*EADING A KICK-ASS WORKFORCE

IN GRADE SCHOOL ONCE, I was struggling to complete an essay-style history test when the class bully tapped me on the shoulder and whispered menacingly, "Mullen! What the hell were the Dark Ages?" I was doomed to trouble, from either my classmate or teacher.

Since the subject of leadership is similarly large and hard to encapsulate, I have provided instead a small collection of management techniques that will both respect employee individuality and encourage organizational improvement.

Therefore, at its best, this chapter on leadership tips will function like an archaeological dig, yielding insights and clues rather than a fully constituted city. At worst, I suppose, it will resemble a flea market whose curious stock is often more desirable to the offerer than the offeree. With luck, something valuable will emerge.

*Fewer is better:* Don't let success go to your head. If you started lean, stay lean. Monitor the amount of time each employee spends in direct contact with either your product or your customers, then question every job in which an outward focus constitutes less than a major part of any day. Nothing drags down an entrepreneurship faster than a proportional shift in the workforce, from line employees (those involved in your customers' businesses) to staff (those dedicated to the operation of your own organization). The steady tracking of indices such as the changes in average salary and income per employee will provide early warning signals of growing bureaucracy.

The concept of adding value by reducing volume gave me the opportunity for a delicious encounter in 1969 with Tom Watson, former chairman of all-powerful IBM. I was sailing aboard *Red Rooster,* one of the three offshore racing yachts that represented the United States in the twenty-nation Admiral's Cup, sailed traditionally in the Solent, the English

Channel, and the Irish Sea. A second boat in our team was Watson's *Palawan*.

At the request of Ted Hood, I was delivering to *Palawan* one of the prototypes of the Hood loft's ultralightweight half-ounce spinnakers, constructed out of the very sheer nylon fibers used to weave women's hosiery. When I encountered the great industrialist in *Palawan*'s cockpit, I passed over this unprepossessing sailbag with its rather princely price tag. Watson weighed the bag in his hand a moment, then gruffly observed, "Rather a lot of money for not much sail, wouldn't you say?"

"It is, Mr. Watson," I replied mischievously, "but if Ted could have built it even lighter, I'd bet he could have charged you more."

*Love is all you need:* One of the most important things I took away from my college experience was a lesson learned in the Holy Cross cafeteria. Most kids treated the minimum-wage luncheon ladies indifferently. I treated them like queens, knowing that the size of their serving was usually proportional to the generosity of my smile. "I love the way you make sandwiches," I'd say as a pudgy hand reached for the pile of sliced ham. "And while you're at it, could I have a little extra cheese and maybe a few more tomatoes on the side? Boy, is that beautiful! Any chance for another handful of chips?"

The moral of the story is that the world is underloved. Make people feel special and they will do special things for you. I tell every new client two secrets to getting the best out of our company: form personal relationships with the people who have the hands-on responsibility for making your ads; and when these people do something very well, thank them publicly, preferably in a note with copies to all the top agency executives and senior client management.

Long ago, I learned that managers can't *make* employees do anything—at least not for very long, and certainly not very well. To achieve a consistent interest in quality, employees have to *want* to do their jobs. I could bellow and bluster all day about the urgency of some vital project, but the moment I left the room every art director and copywriter would go right back to working on a project for the client who had recently showered them with real, knowledgeable appreciation. Our client Mike Rich with *Money* magazine leaves voice-mail messages that are so touchingly beautiful his creative team doesn't erase them for weeks. They save and replay Mike's appreciative comments for family and friends and use them as verbal balm to soothe the wounds inflicted by his less thoughtful (and less effective) peers.

In the early days of the agency, I applied this tactic for a more urgent commercial advantage: to pacify bill collectors. Most managers who owe money do everything possible to ignore messages from harassing accounts-receivable clerks. If these callers finally do catch up with the tardy payer, it's standard procedure for the injured executive to vent loudly about the unappreciative attitude of his vendor.

In contrast, I always called bill collectors right back, asking for them enthusiastically by name, then making happy smalltalk while I pretended to be looking for my copy of the invoice. No matter how sour these accounts-receivable clerks acted, I treated them with great courtesy and respect, if not out-and-out warmth and affection. When, at last, our conversation got down to the main subject—the date on which I was going to make good on a very old obligation—I'd sportingly agree to send 10 percent or so out that same day, half more out in two weeks, and the rest by the end of the month, even if I was liquid enough to pay the whole invoice immediately.

Then I'd attach happy little personal notes to each payment and fastidiously meet the promised schedule, to the day and to the dollar.

The net effect of this practice was that, over time, these clerks learned that they could count on me and our company for a little human warmth and (ultimately) reliable payment. In the meantime, our company's cash-flow benefited enormously from convenient amounts of available funds. For years, our entire agency growth was financed out of our deferred trade payables, with the conspiratorial assistance of an army of normally sour accounts-receivable clerks. I'd like to think it was a mutualism: The underloved clerks' goodwill kept us financially viable; our appreciation brought rare moments of humanity to a thankless job.

*The three steps of persuasion:* All passionate employees will protest management's rejection of a favorite idea, even when it can be shown that the concept doesn't work. At times like these, it's important to not just blow past your employees' objections with a show of authority, but to persuade them with your logic. The first requirement of persuasion is to get the other person to listen.

It amazes me how often good managers miss opportunities to use disagreements to teach important lessons because they don't first take the time to assure the argumentative employee that he's an okay person with an okay point of view. I believe that all persuasion has to be managed in three sequential steps:

(1) *I heard what you have to say:* When the employee voices an objection, don't immediately snap back with your rebuttal. Take a moment to repeat aloud the concern you just heard, rephrasing it ever so slightly to demonstrate that you understand the other person's point of view.

(2) *I think that what you have to say is important:* Don't just echo back the employee's argument, but comment on its relevance and the urgency of addressing that concern. Find a way to point out how important the subject is and how appreciative you are that the employee raised it.

(3) *Now here's my answer to your objection:* Only after you have reassured your employee that he and his points are important can you expect him to be open to your reasoning. In truth, answering your employee's objection may not have required that much serious thought, but you'll find, because you have gone through the first two steps, he will now give

you a chance to change his mind. By honoring your employee with a demonstrable exhibit of listening and caring, you have raised the dynamics of the discussion from autocratic management to a discussion between peers.

By the way, this system also works with clients.

*Motivating, not criticizing:* Once in a while, even the best of employees will develop a bad habit—one, perhaps, that works against the core values of the organization. It's very difficult for a manager to address this kind of problem without seeming to devalue everything else the person has accomplished. Your practical arguments about such things as loss of corporate efficiencies will be overwhelmed by the productive employee's tally of his infinitely more significant contributions. What begins as gentle guidance can suddenly escalate into a fight.

Use a more emotional approach, one that takes advantage of the employee's inherent loyalty and care, and leverages those qualities to motivate him to change. After pointing out the problem, I speak more personally: "You know, John, if it were some of the other people in your group, I might get angry. But you—you're one of our best people. How do you think it makes me *feel* when a person I trust so much does something like this?"

No one can argue about your feelings, and employees who respect you will become very uncomfortable at the thought that they have let you down. Moreover, their resolve to repair that breach of confidence automatically fixes the problem.

*Understanding and meeting the press:* Journalists see themselves as watchdogs who are preserving one of democracy's most important tenets: the public's right to know. Most, in fact, care passionately about the truth and will go to elaborate lengths to honor and serve it. Please allow me to offer a few hard-won nuggets of knowledge for you to use when dealing with the fourth estate.

~ Before you give your first interview, accept the fact that journalists are not there to help you build your career; they're there to report stories that will interest their audience. Unfortunately, what interests audiences most is bad news because we, the public, are more eager to share in the follies of our fellow man than his triumphs. It is ironic how executives who one day rail at the scabrous editorial treatment that they or their companies experienced can be heard the next day clucking over the failings of some other poor victim. As Pogo incisively opined, "We have met the enemy and he is us."

~ Always tell the press the truth. If publishing the truth would be inconsistent with your interests or business standards, learn to construct a dialogue that will convince the journalists of your sincerity but not compromise your integrity. In difficult situations, never answer "no comment." Those two words are to a reporter what a red flag is to a bull. If you truly can't reveal the facts, clearly explain the reasons why and try to provide as much information as possible. The more honest and the more forthcoming you are, the more credibility you will build. In times of difficulty, credibility will be the most important weapon in your arsenal.

Nearly every company that has achieved any level of success has been faced with a life-threatening crisis—a strike, a defective product, a lawsuit, *something*. That crisis will make you and your organization newsworthy, whether you like it or not. Rather than circle the wagons, you should be aggressively open with the press. The reporter can (and will) write the story without your participation, so you should be prepared to represent your side of the discussion as forcefully as possible. When Tylenol and Pepsi Cola experienced high-visibility product sabotage (with potentially disastrous consequences to their brands), both moved quickly and effectively to protect and inform the public. As a result, both emerged as corporate heroes rather than industrial villians.

~ Writers begin each story with an existing point of view. Contemporary journalism requires the press to do more than *report* the news; they must also *interpret* the news. By the time they meet you, therefore, they have already formed many of their opinions on people of your industry, business, race, color, gender, ambition, religion, habit, and preference. When a reporter develops a story that includes you, she will write from her personalized perspective, wrapping facts in preconceptions and drawing conclusions from both. Before you grant the interview, do your best to research the writer's past work for clues on her journalistic themes.

~ No matter how unfairly you think you have been treated by the press, do not make them your enemy. You can never win that war because they always have better weapons. As A.J. Liebling said, "Freedom of the press is limited to those who own one." And Jim Brady added, "Never pick a fight with anyone who buys ink by the barrel."

~ Ultimately, there is no such thing as "off the record." If you say it, journalists have the right to report it. Even if the commitment of confidentiality is actually given, it's standard journalistic practice to check with other sources to find out if the story can be confirmed. Once someone else acknowledges the same information you revealed, the reporter is free to print your secret.

Be aware than an interviewer's openness and friendliness is no indicator of her intentions. The roughest and least fair story ever written about our agency was the product of a man who acted sweet as honey.

~ Never fool yourself that no one really reads or cares about the trade press. The effect on your employees and competitors of an unflattering article in your industry's bible will be temporary, but its influence will drag on for years. Reporters writing for the powerful *consumer* press will dig out that story the day they decide that something about you is worthy of coverage. With the power of computerized editorial searches, journalists can track down all the gamey tidbits that have ever appeared about you or your organization and then requote them with the unassailable authority of the Ten Commandments. Therefore, treat the staff reporter of the most minor trade book or hometown newspaper with the same care and courtesy you would reserve for Dan Rather. Even journalists are only human, and humans have long memories. Besides, you never know where that young writer will turn up next.

~ The press *love* to attack their own darlings. The higher the pedestal on which they place a person, the more tempting she becomes as a target. Cyril Connolly of *The Paris Review* once wrote, "Those

whom the gods wish to punish they first call
'promising.' "

~ Remember also that conversations in public places
are the source of many news stories. Journalists not
only come equipped with the standard complement
of spouses, cousins, and neighbors, but an unusually
wide circle of professional aquaintances eager to
curry favor. If you don't want something in the
press, don't say it publicly, nor to anyone who isn't
a trusted intimate.

Let me illustrate this last point with a story that, while not
involving the press, demonstrates the importance of circum-
spection. Goodby, Silverstein and Partners, one of America's
greatest agencies, was involved in a pitch for the $50 million
IBM PC business. All competitive agency presentations were
being conducted the same day at a hotel meeting room, so the
Goodby team—one of the first to present—arrived the prior
afternoon. In the elevator that evening, a member of the
Goodby creative staff spoke passionately about how he hoped
not to be forced to sit too near any of the IBM computer
nerds, as he really couldn't relate to those kinds of people.

Only when the agency team walked into the presentation room the next day did they learn that they had shared the elevator, and their opinions, with the prospective clients.

Predictably, IBM chose another agency.

# 11

## $\mathscr{K}$EEPING THE WORKFORCE
### KICK-ASS

UNFORTUNATELY, hiring is inherently a flawed process. At the same time the candidate is selling you on his
skills, you are selling the prospective employee on your company. Accept from the outset that, occasionally, things will
not work out. When that happens, face the music and fire the
employee—fire him with compassion, but end the misery for
both of you. What that same person accomplished in earlier
organizations is irrelevant, as are your hopes that with enough
patience the magic will return. As G.E.'s Jack Welch says,
"Deal with reality as it is today, not as it used to be in the past
or as you might want it to be in the future."

Firing an employee is rarely a happy experience.

(Although I did hear about two managers in another company, vying for the privilege of firing a particularly offensive subordinate; as the more senior stated, "The only reason I don't want to fire this guy immediately is because I want to torture him first.") Yet a termination can be done in a way that is fair, reasonable, and believe it or not, even motivating for the rest of your staff. Any manager can live with success. You will show your employees how good you are by the way you handle your failures.

No one can really say how much time a manager should allow to pass before firing an unsuccessful employee, but, for sure, it's more than a few months and less than a year. Most new employees settle down, learn the ropes, and reveal their true personalities—skills and quirks—in under six months. In the event that you're disappointed at that time, odds are excellent that the new employee is as well. Don't wait—start the process that will either turn the situation around or allow you and your unsuccessful hire to part with understanding and dignity.

I've found that in firing an unsuccessful employee, as in all business and personal situations, the truth is the most powerful tool in a manager's arsenal. At an early stage—at least three months before the termination—a good manager will have a clear, open discussion with the failing employee. It's critical that both people have the chance to comment on what's wrong and why, and that together they agree on ways to make things work better. If you feel comfortable that the work environment is supportive and encouraging, then the ultimate responsibility for success lies with the employee. Nonetheless, the manager has to be deeply committed to that employee's achievement of their mutual goals and serious about trying to help.

In the event that the results remain unsatisfactory (and, sadly, they sometimes will), a very clear advisory must be given one solid month before termination, so that the failing employee can become emotionally prepared for what now looms as almost inevitable. Also, without fail, prudence dictates that you review all the legal implications of this firing:

~ Is there a written employment agreement, specifying details of termination?

~ Has the subject of termination been reviewed in an employee manual, or a memo, or even a conversation?

~ Have there been any written or verbal promises of
  job security (particularly if the employee has passed
  up other offers)?

~ Does the employee belong to a protected class:

  over 40?

  non-white?

  pregnant?

  mentally or physically disabled?

~ Has the employee ever complained to management
  about the company's business practices or acts that
  he believes are illegal (in other words, is he a
  whistle-blower)?

If you anticipate trouble, talk with an experienced labor
attorney. While it may cost you a few thousand dollars in fees
and settlement expenses, it could cost you tens or even hundreds of thousands more to litigate a difficult case. Given
juries' prejudices toward "victims" these days, the odds are
stacked pretty heavily in the employee's favor.

Even if none of the usual cautions apply, it's always useful
to follow each pre-termination discussion with a note for the
file, as not all negative reactions happen immediately. Gore

Vidal observed that, after fifty, litigation replaces sex, but the common occurrence of lawsuits following terminations of people in every age group makes me fret for the social adventuresomeness of our younger generations.

Usually, when the day of termination comes, a well-warned employee will actually volunteer the outcome himself. If he doesn't, don't get into an argument with him. Just deliver the bad news as calmly and kindly as possible, and do it in his office, not yours, with the door closed. Avoid both apology and undue praise. If you're concerned about a volatile reaction, ask another senior colleague to be present as a witness. When you're finished, leave the terminated employee alone. Five minutes in private to regain composure, or make a phone call, removes both the incentive and the opportunity for the fired employee to create a messy scene.

Only in the rarest cases, with the most unusual people, should you allow a fired employee to remain at the company after his termination. It's best to ask the terminated person to turn in his keys and security cards and leave right away, making arrangements to help him clean out the personal things from his office the following weekend. Have a trusted (but uninvolved) associate meet him on that Saturday to help—

and, of course, to prevent mischief. It's normal for a person who was terminated on Friday to be pretty burned up about things one morning later. If the fired employee is allowed to linger for days and weeks after he's been given notice, his presence can be bad for everyone's morale. Too much temptation exists for his colleagues and friends to apply the agreeable balm of anti-management dissension, and this will only sow the seeds for future employee problems. Trust that if you have terminated wisely, the people in your company will know it and respect your decision, even if they need to manifest their empathy with a short period of public mourning.

Immediately (by open of business the next day), put a note on the bulletin board that advises your other employees of the change. The message can be truthfully kind ("Changes in the Amalgamated Confetti account require our company to downsize our service staff. . . .") or kindly euphemistic ("Sally has left to pursue her interests in . . ."). Never be a bulletin board bully by discussing the fired employee's shortcomings publicly, but don't apologize for the action you've taken either. Firing is as much your job as hiring, and you don't need to appeal for public vindication.

It's easy to feel awash with relief when the terminated

employee actually walks out the door and out of your life, and to bend your mind to solving other problems. It's also not very smart to forget about this situation so quickly. In reality, you are turning loose a person who is an expert witness on your organization, who will either testify to the world in your behalf or to your detriment. With a little effort—a more generous severance package than necessary, active assistance in finding a new job, telephone calls of support, employment references that truthfully concentrate on the fired person's positives—it is amazing how a person you fired can become an advocate for the company and remain a walking testimonial to the fairness and compassion of your corporate culture.

I suppose I've developed this heightened sensitivity to firing with grace because the first such event I ever witnessed was one of the most horrific imaginable.

At my first real (non-lab, non-charter boat) job in the customer service department of the yacht hardware company, terminations were not rare, but rarely were they this colorful. A young, ambitious expediter I shall call Phil was elevated to a minor management position, moving him out of the ranks of gray metal desks and into one of those doorless steel-and-glass cubicles that resemble an expanded toilet stall (but offer even less privacy). Phil's first official management assignment was to fire a twenty-year-plus employee I'll refer to as Sammy, a diligent, partially deaf inventory clerk whose function had become redundant. By four-thirty that day, the fifty of us in the gray-desk squadron were primed to witness the event that only poor Sammy didn't know was to happen.

Phil called; Sammy entered and sat, unaware that this day was to be any different from the last seven thousand he gave the company. "Sammy," Phil stammered, "management has decided to phase out the manual inventory system, and I have to fire you."

"Oh, Phil, that's terrible," the hard-of-hearing Sammy replied, rising from his chair with a look of shock and genuine sympathy. "You've only been a manager one day; how can they fire you without any warning? Look, Phil, I'm an old-timer here. Let me go talk to the president. I think I can help you out."

"No, Sammy, no," Phil shouted in panic, losing all sense of place and cool. "*It's not me! It's you, it's you! You're fired! You're fired! You're fired!*"

# 12

## $\mathcal{S}$ALARIES: HOW TO KNOW HOW MUCH TO PAY

THE SENIOR VICE PRESIDENT of the American Association of Advertising Agencies was furious. I, president of one of the association's emerging high-profile companies, had been secretly photocopying its very private, very confidential report to senior agency management, the annual *Employee Compensation Analysis*, then circulating it among our entire workforce. The result, of course, was that everyone, from our clerks to our mid-level operating people, had access to the real salary data, by title and region, for every job in our industry.

"This is a dangerous and aberrant practice" harrumphed the offended AAAA executive in his most officious Caesar

Augustus manner. "It absolutely terrifies me to have this confidential information fall into the hands of agency employees."

Dangerous and aberrant? Really? I was bewildered by the twisted logic that called for salary structures to remain secret, accessible only to one or two agency executives. Built into this implied conspiracy was the assumption that the bulk of advertising's workforce was blind to their industry's salary structures, something any manager should know is patently ridiculous. I mean, hadn't we hired these people to shepherd our clients' brands and budgets because they were smart? Didn't they get into advertising in the first place because they heard somewhere that it paid eye-popping salaries? Wouldn't most have figured out that a nationally famous creative director makes a whole lot more than a copywriter at the dawn of her career?

All these arguments aside, isn't it reasonable for management to give younger employees a clear, long-term perspective on the financial implications of their chosen professional paths?

"No!" came the unequivocal rumble from the AAAA officer. "What about inequities among pay scales in different departments?" Why, I wondered, are salary differences inequitable? Should the fellow who occasionally taps the triangle in a symphony orchestra be paid at the same level as the first violinist? In our company, when hardworking media planners ask why art directors make more money than they do, I tell them it beats the hell out of me. Maybe it's supply and demand, or maybe it's a universal perception that their contributions have different values. Either way, salary structures are out of my control. I tell frustrated media planners that if they want to make more money, it's simple—they should become art directors.

"But if people find out they're above the mean industry salary, won't you lose control?" challenged the defender of industry secrecy. "And if they're below it, won't you have a revolt on your hands?"

First, people shouldn't be above or below mean salary levels unless there's a very good reason. If the explanation for this deviation is merely management's negotiating weakness at the high end or corporate opportunism in the lower ranges, you bet your life that trouble is on its way. Second, isn't it better for employees to learn what their contributions are really worth from their own company managers rather than from their peers—or, worse yet, from the managers of the company's competitors?

Of all the components that make up a compensation package, salary is invariably the most emotional. Therefore, if your goal is to form a bond of trust with your employees, an equitable salary structure is an important place to start. Salaries should be fair, period. Deciding what's fair, however, is one of the thorniest thickets in business. By its very nature, a company's salary scale offers entrepreneurial managers a superb device for messing up an employee relationship.

In companies where management consciously keeps payroll low, a self-correcting process invariably will take place: The quality of the employees will sink to the level of the inadequate salaries. Slowly, but inexorably, the workforce will bifurcate into two squads—congenital incompetents and malcontent dissemblers. The incompetents will plod robotically through the day, the dissemblers will use their entrepreneurial wiles vengefully to give their organization as little value as possible. Frankly, it's not worth spending much time discussing ways to deal with businesses that are knowingly exploitative. If you have landed in this kind of environment, quit now and use your time to find a more entrepreneurial company. Then come back later to finish this book.

More dangerous, perhaps, are those organizations where salaries are corruptively high. There are many advertising agencies with whom we compete that use what I call the star system of employee compensation, and use it brutally. Whoever is the fresh, hot talent is quickly awarded a new salary at a level startlingly above industry standards. This lofty income has the effect of temporarily stabilizing the star, making her financially untouchable by poaching competitors. Inevitably, however, things change and for one reason or another the star's luster begins to fade. Subtly or unsubtly, the company's management will start to invent a hundred little ways to make her situation untenable. Sooner or later, a new star replaces the old, who nobly "resigns," accompanied by a momentary clucking by the industry press. Then, this make-and-break syndrome is forgotten, until it's repeated, something that happens at regular intervals.

What isn't palpable to industry observers, though, is the havoc this creates in the former star's career and personal life. Count on the fact that, at some point, the star began to believe her own PR and concluded that she was, indeed, God's gift to the industry. And, count on the fact that matching her heroically proportioned salary was a magnificently expansive lifestyle, with all the attendant financial obligations.

Now this former star starts a new job search, certain in her lofty abilities, confident in being universally desired. But time passes and no one hires her, because no rational company will pay the inflated price it takes to meet her financial expectations. Moreover, no one wants to insult an industry heroine with a lowball offer. What has happened, in effect, is that the star's former employer has taken one of its best people— someone who played an important role in creating the organization's fame, its profits, and its equity—and turned her into a personal failure.

I thought about this and decided that the star system was not only inhumane for the employee, but also guaranteed to have a corrosive effect on long-term company profits. In order to keep overall company salary costs proportional to overall income, outrageously high paychecks for a few stars require anemic paychecks for the rest. Fairness aside, the cyclical turmoil of the resulting turnover would devour the time of senior management, the company's most valuable employees. Never does time equal money more than when productive people are spending their day thinking about something other than their clients' businesses.

All logic says that companies don't set salary levels, industries do, and not to recognize this fact is silly for both the employee and the company. Therefore, it makes sense to get hold of a trustworthy industry salary analysis (or any surrogate that reveals compensation structures) and publish it openly among your employees. Yes, that's what I'm suggesting: that senior management actually tell each and every one of the company's employees what their labor is worth on the open market. Moreover, I'm suggesting that management tell them the industry pay scales for every job at every level of the company. (It's interesting that the same American Association of Advertising Agencies, which once took pains to condemn my "dangerous and aberrant practices," today has asked me to be a director, and to speak at regional gatherings all over the country explaining to other agencies how our compensation system works.)

Experience has taught me that most people should be paid somewhere within 20 percent of their industry's interquartile mean (the middle 50 percent), thereby removing the influence of those in the top and bottom quartiles who are paid either way too much or way too little. This system tosses out the salaries of both the overpaid stars and the underpaid exploitees and lets managers compare their employees' salaries against others in the industry who are being competitively compensated. By varying the standard by a full 20 percent, managers can cover most or all of the differentials in the talent and experience of individual workers.

If you seize the initiative and make a practice of distributing information on industry salary standards, you will proactively reassure the company's best people that the grass isn't a demonstrably more verdant hue in your competitors' back forty. These employees will both appreciate your honesty and reciprocate your trust. Moreover, salary standards are a fabulous platform for annual employee-performance discussions, because they require you to set aside all your selling techniques and to quantify the truth. If someone is performing below standards, their salary should reflect this and you should be ready to explain why. In time, all who participate in this experience learn that the financial truth doesn't just set free the minds of honest men and women, it sets free their spirits, encouraging them to be their best.

Our agency once employed a hard-trying traffic manager, essentially a coordinator and expediter of the work by all the in-house specialists and outside suppliers needed to make an ad.

She was sincere and popular, but not overly qualified for her job. Following her disappointing departmental annual review, the traffic manager appealed her tepid raise to me, the court of final resort. "The AAAA's salary report shows that traffic managers make between $23,000 and $25,000," she said, "but I only make $20,000."

"That's because you're not a very good traffic manager," I truthfully responded. "You're not so bad that we want to fire you, but not good enough to pursue administration as a career." When she asked my advice on what she could do to reorient her career in the right direction, I told her I thought she was a very warm and persuasive person and that she ought to explore opportunities to get out of administration and into sales.

My colleague Joe Grimaldi lined up our young traffic manager with a *pro bono* job selling ads to agencies for the Advertising Club of Boston's annual directory. There, she could practice her selling skills in a noncompetitive environ-ment while she was still employed with us. Success in this sales effort led to a series of other account service jobs out-side our company, each building experience and confidence.

Today, she represents a very successful photographer and recently told me that, working part-time (to be home with her young son), she now earns annual commissions that have more than tripled her income. Best of all, we've remained friends.

# 13

## *W*HO REALLY OWNS
## AN ENTREPRENEURIAL COMPANY?

A S   I   L O O K   B A C K at the dysfunctional companies I've known firsthand and those I've bumped up against in my formative business years, I've recognized one common characteristic: each was an organization that was *served by* its employees, not an organization dedicated to *serving* its workforce. The employees, of course, learned the rules of this exploitative game from their employers, and became equally adept at returning the compliment. This sad dynamic of equal and opposite exploitations becomes cultural and inevitably plays out as a management versus managed lifetime tug of war.

From the time I had that pivotal conversation with Steve Haesche about the unfairness he found in other agencies, I became determined to prevent that miserable condition in our company. The first problem with which I wrestled was the struggle that faces every salaried person, the struggle to develop enough equity to face retirement securely. But can any company really provide long term security for every employee? No, probably not, but it could damned well try. At the very least it ought to augment its employees' ability gracefully to manage their sunset years.

The reality is that it's tough for any one of us to save money when living on a salary. This is particularly true in the robust years of an expanding career, when income and expenses seem to spiral effortlessly upward in virtual lockstep, and savings are postponed as tomorrow's luxury. Even in these sober, responsible nineties, we still tend to concentrate our assets in the things that we want or need to sustain our current lives—the house, cars, education for the kids, maybe a few toys, and probably some vacations. Normally, other than the appreciation of our primary residences, we don't accumulate much that builds durable equity. The question isn't whether this spend-for-today attitude is or is not smart thinking on the part of salaried employees; people spend because the necessities or the enticements are so immediate and the consequences of not saving are so distant. Even when spending is patently dumb, life is often so burdensome that the temptation to purchase a little relief is universal and irresistible.

The question that really begs to be addressed is whether the entire entrenched system of corporate ownership is fair. What (or, more poignantly, who) really builds equity within a corporation and how do you measure each builder's contribution?

When I finally reasoned my way to the conclusions that follow, my management of our company's stock suddenly took a left turn. I metamorphosed from a confirmed conservative capitalist to an even more confirmed social pragmatist, a radical enough change that people around me might have concluded that I had suddenly become (gasp) a liberal!

In market-based economies, the principle of ownership has always been closely tied to the concept of financial risk: the person who put up the money owns the object because if the object goes away, the money is gone, too. But what if the object is a growing company whose equity and asset values are expanding? Is the capital invested either by founders or stockholders the only thing that causes the organization's value to appreciate? To me, it seems not. Having been closely associated with a growing company for many years (and *very* closely associated with the capital investment), I have come to the conclusion that it's the contributions of many people that produce the equity, and that these contributions are incremental to the growth created by financial risk.

Certainly, when founders and stockholders continue to be among the people building value into a company as it grows, they deserve not only to hold on to their original share, but also to accrue that equity which they personally create. But any way you cut it, neither the founders nor those who took the initial financial risk are solely responsible for 100 percent of the tangible worth of a growing organization. As the company expands, its appreciation in value increasingly results from the contributions of others.

If I were debating Henry Ford on this subject, I'm sure he would immediately argue that employees get salaries but owners take the risks. After all, Henry might say, aren't all those employees getting *paid* to do the work that creates the stockholder equity? Sure they are, but in an entrepreneurial organization every person is adding a value beyond salary, and rarely are those kinds of contributions recognized. It is my firm belief that as time goes on, an increasing percentage of the equity of any company is actually grown in place, not deposited there as a cash investment by the stockholders or earned exclusively as a result of that money's availability. Therefore, logic says that the percentage of equity the employees create is the percentage they should own.

The benefit of sharing equity actually spreads in two directions: As the employees build equity, they also build commitment. It is very doubtful that Ford's rank and file laborers were then or are now importantly invested in the corporation's interests—an indifference that management resents the same way that labor rankles at supervisory privileges.

Sharing equity doesn't come naturally to any of us. It is much like sharing power, an acquired taste. Those who have founded and built companies can expect to experience a surge of terror as they watch their hard-won percentage of ownership shrink. The problem, of course, is that they're concentrating on the wrong numbers—percentages rather than dollars.

I don't know about you, but I've never been able to spend a percent in my life. I can spend only money. Therefore, I concluded that it would be smarter to concentrate not on the lost *percentages* of the stock that passed out of my hands but on the *cash value* of those shares that remained. Why should I care if there is a dilution of my ownership percentage as long as the value of the residual shares keeps improving at an encouraging rate? It seems to me that it is far better to have a smaller share of a big company than a big share of a small company. Not only are my corporate assets more equitably distributed, they're more secure, because I've linked my fate to the self-interest of a broad group of equally enfranchised associates.

In brief, I concluded that the very best way to get my colleagues to think like owners was to make them owners.

Our company's first equity distribution was through an ESOP, an employee stock ownership plan that purchased 20 percent of the shares from me using funds borrowed from a bank at a discounted rate. (Banks get tax breaks from money earned on ESOP loans, and are usually willing to share the benefit by loaning money to the corporation more cheaply for that purpose.) The ESOP then distributes stock annually to all qualified employees—in our case, those with more than a year of service.

Frankly, our early ESOP distributions were not particularly motivating, especially to the young people in our young company. Each person's original number of shares was tiny, and the stock wasn't worth very much. But as the company grew every year, the stock increased in value, and every year all qualified employees got a little more, without fanfare and without cost. As the calendar changed, nickels piled on top of nickels to become thousands of dollars that, compounded by our company's consistent growth rates, have developed into a significant cash hedge against retirement for a large percentage of our people. Today, many employees in our agency have ESOP stock valued at tens of thousands of dollars; a few have much more. This equity was acquired untaxed and without having to be snatched each year from each employee's normal salary income. Whether an employee's share is ultimately worth a few thousand or a few hundred thousand dollars, it will be available to her and her family in cash upon retirement, when her tax obligations will be at their lowest. For many, it may well be the amount that will help them to enjoy retirement without worry.

I remember the weird experience of meeting with the financial specialist who set up our original ESOP. The expert spent the first hour telling me how ESOPs were designed to work, gleefully chortling about all the little devices his other clients used to make sure most of their employees never really qualified for the payout. Using this expert's method, the ESOP became a great device for tax-deferred income for—guess who?—the founder of the business. I not only persistently ignored his recommendations but insisted on my own special conditions: an income salary skew so that the distributions are driven toward the lower end of the payroll; employee participation after one year with the company; 100 percent vesting after only seven years of employment.

"Wait a minute, I get it," this astonished financial guru finally blurted out, "you want an ESOP that really works like an ESOP!" And one wonders why employees are suspicious of management.

At a number of points during the last few years, I have also assessed the equity positions of key company builders and asked myself, "Are these proportions fair?" Sometimes the intellectually honest answer has been yes, but on a few occasions it's been otherwise. A few years ago, I was riding in a car with our chief creative officer, Paul Silverman, and speculating on the number of his stock options, which, by my reckoning, gave him rights to a substantial percent of the shares outstanding. "But I don't have that much," said Paul, citing a much smaller number.

"Impossible," I assured him—but a quick check back at the office revealed he was right. That same day, I reviewed the distribution of ownership in our company and granted additional blocks of options not only to Paul but to several other key contributors to our growth.

For the last five years, I have also issued a discretionary amount of stock options to each of our company's officers (those with titles of vice president or higher) under a nonqualified stock option plan with options vesting over seven years. As each portion came up for purchase, the grantee could elect to exercise his option and buy that stock at a favorable price, one third the share value the day the grant was issued. All did, and all have been rewarded by substantial company and equity growth.

Over the years, we have changed our system of equity distribution several times, always with the intention of making it fairer and more motivational. Today, we also need to cure some problems that have ended up penalizing the company financially and burdening our most productive people with unnecessary taxes.

The options granted to key employees were originally issued at a value of $0.01—essentially free—while today our stock is valued at about $60 per share. Each year 10 percent of those options become vested, making the option holders liable for the taxes on their full value (our current share price less one cent). In recognition of their contributions, the company covered this cost for them. When the tax laws of 1993 sharply raised marginal rates to 43.19 percent for highly paid executives, paying these taxes became a very expensive proposition.

Worse yet, the company was required to accrue as an expense the full value of the exercised options. By 1994 this hit to the books, combined with the cash for the taxes, was costing the company hundreds of thousands of dollars—money that could be added to our profit-sharing.

The problems with the officers' options were similar. Even though officers could purchase stock at only one-third of par value it took post-tax dollars to do so, not always a comfortable expenditure for people with family demands. Here again the company was required to accrue an expense equal to the other two-thirds of the stock purchase, more money that could be part of our profit-sharing pool.

We're solving these problems in several ways:

~ All unvested options now will vest on each person's normal retirement date or time of death, eliminating both the current taxes and hit to the company's books.

~ All new options are issued at fair market value and are exercisable at the time of normal retirement, death, or voluntarily if there is an internal offer to purchase. When the options vest and are sold, the employee pays the taxes only on the *growth* of the stock; the purchase has no effect on the company's books.

~ The company now contributes more aggressively to the ESOP which, in turn, can purchase shares from me, the grantees and the officers at capital gains tax rates (about half the rate of ordinary income). It can also purchase options if the holders are willing to endure the tax at ordinary income rates. Essentially, I allow others to offer as many shares for sale as they choose and then modulate the market by tendering only some of mine. This way I make sure that I'm not the dominant benefactor of the ESOP's purchase.

It is my intention to boost the ESOP's ownership significantly, allowing it to acquire stock for our employees' retirement and, at the same time, create a market for stock owned by the larger shareholders. Ultimately, it is my dream to build a fully liquid internal market where shares can be bought and sold no differently than they are on the public exchange. This isn't a fantasy. The $1.7 billion Science Applications International has a booming private market right now—and began it when they were just our size.

It's obvious that with enough grants, enough options, and enough time, a founder such as myself someday will slip into a minority ownership position. That, of course, is exactly the object of the exercise. I not only receive the incremental income from each year's stock sale while I'm still young enough to enjoy it, but, presumably, my remaining minority shares are worth an ever-increasing amount of money. What often prevents founders from doing the right thing with equity distribution is the specter that in becoming a minority stockholder, they could involuntarily be tossed out of the company they toiled and risked to form—a situation that would make any reasonable leader paranoid. My solution to this problem was to declare that all options awarded to key employees and purchased through nonqualified options programs would be non-voting. With these voting rights secured in my hands, I can rest comfortably in my minority position without the fear of a palace coup.

But what of paranoia on the other side of the equation, among the other equity-holding employees? If I hold most of the cards, can they ever feel completely secure about the liquidity of their ownership? What if I were to sell my shares and the control of the company without any consideration for the non-voting shareholders? Couldn't the other shareholders all end up working for a stranger—someone who might, ultimately, give them no way to cash out their equity in the agency? This is not an unreasonable concern, particularly if the employees, collectively, hold a majority of the shares outstanding—most of which is non-voting.

I addressed this by building into all stock distribution plans a condition known as "Parallel Exit." In essence, this requires that in the event I ever dispose of all or even a large block of my stock, the other shareholders and option holders will be treated equally: They will be entitled to exactly the same deal at exactly the same moment in time. Therefore, if I abruptly and indiscriminately sell my shares to a larger agency, the cash received can't just be used to buy my stock. All options would vest immediately and the buyer's cash will be used to redeem the stock of every person in our company, proportional to that person's ownership. If the purchase payment is some combination of cash and stock in the acquirer's corporation, each of our company's equity holders will receive exactly the same proportion of cash and new shares as I do, and receive them on exactly the same schedule. In short my self-interest is tied directly to that of my employees, and theirs is tied to mine. The principle of fairness holds, no matter what. We built the company together, and—win or lose—we will share its assets together.

Perhaps the greatest benefit of this system for a privately held company is that it allows the founders and major stockholders to convert their stock into cash over a period of time. The ESOP buys the founder's shares as well as those of the grantees and officers as their options mature. Slowly but inexorably, the older managers are getting out—without selling the company to a third party and, simultaneously, selling its long-term employees down the river. Moreover, the system allows new leaders to emerge from within and then to cash out their equity while redistributing the control to the next generation.

In summary, this somewhat complex, capitalistically pragmatic, socialistically equitable system of corporate ownership has five extremely useful values to the company and all those whose careers are involved in its growth:

1. It motivates key entrepreneurial employees because it allows them to build corporate equity without being forced to start their own spinoff companies (with, usually, employees and clients from the original).

2. The process by which shares vest over time makes it harder for emerging leaders to jump ship, thereby giving up the predictable growth in the stock programs of your organization to follow the siren song of a competitor operating on the star system.

3. It allows the older stockholders to reduce their equity slowly, for cash, as the company is growing.

4. It creates an automatic structure for succession since, when the founder does leave the company, a few key players will have already achieved a controlling interest.

5. It increases the likelihood that the company will

continue after the founder has left, without requiring a purchase by an outside party.

I am so concerned about establishing a company equity structure that has a fighting long-term chance to continue to provide fulfilling and happy lives for those who build and sustain the company's goals that I've actually gone one step further. My will specifies that the heir to my stock is the company itself, and, indirectly, the people who have done the most to make my life worth living.

By way of outrageous contrast, let me illustrate how differently the process of succession can be. I once worked with a small silk-screen printing company whose current owner had purchased the business from its founder, a quiet craftsman who, because it was part of his buyout agreement, was forced to remain as the head of the creative group. It seems that the artisan and former owner had suffered a severe heart attack in his early forties and decided that the nine-to-five routine of cutting screens for his successor was preferable to the prospect of ongoing stress and further health problems. In retrospect, only the decision to sell was right; the decision to stay was disastrous.

The person to whom he sold the business, now his new boss, was a soap-opera version of the archetypical high-pressure businessman, raging through each day as if he had swallowed a whole bottle of steroids. The pair clashed often, and I wasn't exactly one hundred percent sure the environment provided peaceful therapy for a red-ticket heart patient. One afternoon, the human Doberman who now was running the shop accosted me in his office, blazing with unrequited fury. "Did you hear what my chief screen cutter did to me?" he shouted. "He died!"

All I could do was gasp, "That ungrateful SOB," before fleeing, in horror, forever.

# 14

## PROFITS:
## THE MORE YOU GIVE AWAY,
## THE MORE YOU SEEM TO KEEP

IF ARISTOTLE WAS the most brilliant philosopher of his era, Watergate's Deep Throat was the most penetrating of ours. "If you want to know how things work," he told Bob Woodward, "follow the money." Sadly, if you follow the money in most organizations, it leads right to senior management. Sooner or later, managers have to ask themselves a serious question: Where is the best place for an organization to invest its profits?

In the first half of this book, I championed the power of psychic rewards to motivate employees, and those principles remain the cornerstones of my beliefs. Undeniably, however, money can act as an urgent catalyst, increasing both the reactive speed and reaction depth of an entrepreneurial mixture that already has combustive ingredients.

The previous chapters dealt with equity and salaries, two of the three weapons available in your financial arsenal. Yet while reasonable paychecks and accrued equity may raise your employees' consciousness about the fairness of your organization, I'm sorry to report that neither is going to create the real driving energy behind employee motivation and company growth. A market-based salary is regulated by supply and demand, and equity appreciation is limited by the fact that, in a growing company, each year's distribution is shared by more and more people. Nonetheless, your employee's total compensation packages do not have to be so tightly constrained. There is a third mechanism available to you, perhaps the most powerful of all.

In our company, the entrepreneurial flame became a bonfire when I extended the principle of fairness to the ultimate in employee enfranchisement: full disclosure of all the financial details of our company and full employee participation in all the resulting profits. I am convinced that, more than fair salaries and distributed equity, it is the opportunity to share in the company's profits that will inspire employees to create organizational wealth—by working harder to generate new income, by thinking smarter before spending the company's resources.

The theory behind profit sharing is brutally simple and elegantly effective: individuals become committed to the company's success when it is linked directly to their own personal finances.

At the outset of every fiscal year, our financial analysts project our anticipated salary and overhead costs, then add whatever retained earnings the company will need to smooth its cash flow and to finance its ongoing growth. Since retained earnings are the profit that stays within the company to build its working capital, the company also must provide for the taxes necessary to hang on to that obligatory nest egg.

Together, salaries, overhead, retained earnings, and taxes constitute the annual nut that must be cracked for the company to remain healthy and viable. But after our agency achieves a level of income sufficient to cover these costs, every bit of incremental profit—I mean *every* dollar, dime, and penny—is shared in cash among all employees, proportional to the contribution each has made that year. It didn't take long for the implications of this system to sink in among our workforce and for the effect to permeate every income-generating and spending decision every employee makes every day.

Consider it from the employees' point of view. Where does the money come from to pay for an hour-long call to Aunt Gertrude in Hawaii, to ship something by Federal Express that could go via surface mail, or to hire that decorative but unnecessary assistant? Not from salaries, because they're set by the industry; not from retained earnings, because the future stability of the company is sacred; and not from taxes because, well ... you know. Money wasted by employees can come from only one place—the pool of profits to be shared among all in the organization. Waste is no longer something that is absorbed by a faceless corporation; waste is something that erodes the income of every person in the workforce. The principle isn't very deep; employees will treat the company's money as their own *when it really is*.

Conversely, where does the additional company income go that resulted from all those employee late nights, sacrificed weekends, and missed vacations? Or the extra care that everyone who touched the product took to make it better and more saleable? Not to the bonuses of a greedy senior management, because all employees are rewarded proportionally, including the top people in the company. And not into the paychecks of some agency star, because the company has fairness mechanisms that discourage this kind of desperate salary structure. Incremental income becomes part of the profit sharing pool that is owned collectively by all employees, the very people who put the value there in the first place.

The first step to making this theory work is a company policy of open books. Management must be willing to share all the consolidated financial information with every employee, regardless of title, position, or years of service. On a quarterly basis, our entire staff meets in the early evening to review the previous three months' income and expense figures and to hear how they are projected to affect the year-end results. Attendance at these meetings is voluntary, but people who miss for no good reason are few. (For those people unable to schedule free time on the designated evening, there's usually a synopsized makeup presentation a day or so later.) In addition to providing the venue for a company-wide financial discussion, these quarterly meetings become great places to make major announcements, such as promotions or the introduction of new agency personnel, and to listen to the questions employees have about how the agency's business actually works.

At the meeting that kicks off the first quarter of our new fiscal year, we begin by reviewing all the gross numbers necessary to give an accurate projection of where the company stands financially, projected for the upcoming twelve months. As with most companies who have survived long enough to have some sort of historical perspective, we're very good at forecasting expenses—aggregate salaries and projected overhead costs. Therefore, de facto, we can calculate the next year's income required for us to comfortably pay our salaries and the associated overhead costs. To these anticipated annual expenses I add whatever retained corporate earnings I believe will be necessary to keep our company strong, and to that, painfully, whatever amount will be necessary to cover our resulting federal and state taxes.

The proper level of retained earnings is not a subject for agency-wide debate or even discussion. It's a function of such things as our balance sheet, banking relations, planned equipment purchases, and facility expansion plans—areas of responsibility that are uniquely mine. Therefore, that judgment also is mine since, in the world of rights and responsibilities, it is my obligation to see that our books remain healthy. Strong financials are what provide our company the elasticity to survive difficult periods and what keep the job of every person in our company secure.

When, at the year's opening meeting, we total up our salaries, overhead costs, required retained earnings, and the associated taxes, it becomes pretty clear that if we cannot achieve a corresponding operating profit, our company will have to make cuts either in staff or overhead. Everyone in the organization understands up front what our minimum level of success must be, and everyone knows the consequences of not achieving it.

Since advertising is a volatile industry, projecting the new year's income is a whole lot harder than forecasting the upcoming twelve months of expenses. The income forecasts on which we rely are the honest, cumulative opinions of the line managers for each of our accounts, those in the best position to make accurate judgments. History shows that these projections are conservative, encouraging us to keep expenses equally restrained thereby reducing the potential for an end-of-the-year surprise.

Since forecasting is an area of frequent management abuse, it's worth emphasizing that this process totally relies on employee judgments. We never encourage our account directors to plump their report with optimism to satisfy an agency objective, or to lower their projections so as to be heroes when they exceed expectations. In fact, we don't even rely on our written client contracts; we ask our managers to use their best judgment to forecast what, in their opinions, really is likely to happen. Since our account services staff are the people closest to the clients, it stands to reason that they will have the best feel about which relationships and contractual income are solid and which might be shaky. In no case do we forecast income that is not either tied to a signed contract or otherwise positively assured by a reliable client. Verbal approvals can be forecasted, but not unspecific intentions. This discipline is important. Since we are always working against a projection that is highly probable, we never mislead ourselves into thinking that the future year's forecast is rosier than reality.

The most common and most abusive forecasting practice is the system of quotas, whereby employees are assigned aggressive management-established monthly revenue targets, regardless of what the market can naturally yield. This only teaches those responsible to play games with money. In order to deliver on unreliably high promises, employees are forced to complete sales at all costs, including circumstances when more volume will yield poor profits and even compromise the brand. Conversely, when sales are better than anticipated, employees are tempted to tone down forecasts as a hedge against the erosion of other accounts.

Worse yet, sales pressures often contravene a customer's best interests and this is guaranteed, someday, to be deadly. No forced sales gains are worth the tension and distraction they cause the company's managers, and no monthly profit objective is worth compromising the confidence of a long term client relationship.

At our first quarter (Q1) company meeting, all our forecasted income figures are arrayed against the more certain projections of salary and overhead costs, retained earnings, and taxes. For us, this initial collision of anticipated income and outgo is seemingly disastrous: Invariably their resolution indicates that our company should expect to sustain a serious loss for the upcoming year. Yet this doesn't seem to frighten any of our employees (except, perhaps, me). By way of buoying up myself and everyone else, I compare the loss projected for our upcoming year with the equally terrifying initial projections from the last five years. It is comforting to see that in each our initial dismal forecast was transformed to actual year-end results that included both profits and profit sharing. History argues for optimism at each new beginning.

Still, the direness of our initial prediction makes everyone in the room realize it won't be easy for our company to achieve its retained earnings and go on to build a wholesome level of profit sharing. Each year it takes work, and lots of it. Sometimes I suspect that our veterans actually enjoy the prospect of their annual uphill battle toward prosperity.

To understand how our costs compare to those of similar organizations, we use industry figures tabulated in the AAAA's *Annual Analysis of Agency Costs* to check our detailed line-item expenses against our competitors'. Variances below industry norms are seen as victories, not permission to spend more in that area during the year ahead. Variances above industry norms are carefully scrutinized in light of our agency practices, culture, and objectives. Many apparent overages upon investigation turn out to be the result of good decisions and not careless management. For instance, our new business costs always run higher than ad industry averages but, then again, so does our capture rate for the accounts we pitch. Who can argue with high new business expenses if they produce a continuous stream of fresh opportunities?

In my experience, the best way to cut costs in a category where expenses appear to be out of line is to discuss the situation openly in a quarterly meeting, then ask the entire employee group to do something about it. I tend not to talk with the specific individuals or departments who are responsible for the unusual bulge in costs, and I try never to offer suggestions on how economies should be achieved. Instead, I talk to the entire workforce so that everyone knows both the problem and the people responsible for fixing it. There is nothing like peer pressure to get the responsible people to eliminate costly excesses.

Over the years, I've learned that when motivated employees understand they are causing waste, understand its high cost and understand that they are covering these wasteful expenses with their own profit-sharing cash, it is quite astonishing how fast the appropriate cuts are made.

At each of the year's first three quarterly meetings, I review the financial events of the previous three months and update all the end-of-the-year projections. Invariably, income begins to rev up and expenses decline as the economies kick in from the continuous employee drive to reduce waste. As the year marches on, it becomes irresistibly exciting for us all to see how our communal efforts are making good financial things happen. These swelling income numbers and the declining cost figures reinforce the confidence that we have in ourselves and our colleagues.

About halfway through the year, we always seem to hit the magic figure—sufficient income to cover our salaries, overhead, retained earnings and taxes. From that moment forward, every nickel of additional income we bring in and every penny of costs we can cut belongs to all employees. It isn't a question anymore of *if* we are going to share profits; it's only a question of how much. The answer to that question is in the hands of the company's workforce.

Since our company has a fiscal year that begins in September, our fourth quarter extends from June through August— traditionally the doldrums of the advertising business. Yet four years out of five, our agency's fourth quarter has been its most profitable period. While the industry's business may be slacking off in summertime, our employee motivation is peaking. The fact that the final size of our profit-sharing pool is a direct function of employee commitment offers a strong incentive for the entire workforce to close out the year with a bang.

In the dozen years that this system has been in effect, we've never had anything less than great results. We always earn profits comfortably in the top third of our industry (but not so high as to indicate that we are pricing ourselves out of the market). Equally important, we can demonstrate to our clients that this profitability yields employee stability, a characteristic that translates directly into the steady, uninterrupted staffing of their accounts.

All of the above presumes success, with succeeding quarters each spawning the glory of the next. Unfortunately, life is not always thus. There have been quarters that I have delivered sobering financial news to our employees. Once our first half figures were so bad that I was required to make the direst correction of all, a six person layoff. Our people could accept this bad news because they understood the reasons behind it; no authority speaks more eloquently than the financial truth. When I spelled out the fiscal realities, the reasons for our layoff became obvious. Equally obvious was the fact that additional layoffs would not be necessary. Because they knew the truth, both good and bad, our remaining people could get on with their jobs without further dis-traction. The wonderful thing is that our year's second half was a gangbuster, and we ended the year with solid profits and robust profit sharing.

One could question if this system of open books could work in a company that's either a profitless start-up or one that is in significant financial trouble. In these cases, the con-cept of profit sharing is moot: with no near-term possibility of surplus earnings, there is no realistic prospect of extra employee income. My answer is yes. I believe the same system *will* work in organizations that are temporarily financially stressed, because the system's emphasis is less on realizing incremental income and more on telling the employees the financial truth. When employees are part of the process, they become part of the solution.

Sooner or later, every employee-oriented company will become profitable and will need a fair system for the distribu-tion of the employees' shares. Our agency's method of deter-mining each individual's portion is, not surprisingly, management's best judgments—mine among the senior man-agers, those of Paul Silverman and Joe Grimaldi among the departments. With this rough cut in hand, we invite other key associates to help fine-tune the share of profits in their areas of responsibility, since our line managers work more closely with the employees than even Paul and Joe.

I begin the distribution process by taking a large dollop of the profit-sharing pool (more or less two-thirds of the cash available) and with the help of a computer spreading it evenly across our employee base as a fixed percent of the actual total salary paid to each that fiscal year. (Calculating actual money paid rather than annualized salary removes the inequities of partial-year employment and mid-year salary changes.) In a good year (and most are), this initial profit-sharing allocation will represent between 15 and 25 percent of every individual's actual pay.

The reason I begin with salaries is that if the company's pay scale is fair, payroll ought to be the best indicator of proportional contribution. With the advantage of hindsight, though, managers will recognize that some people deserved higher salaries. Therefore, we correct this inequity by then taking the remaining third (or so) of the profit-sharing pool and apply it judiciously to our outstanding employees, directly introducing merit into the distribution equation. It may sound silly, but I like adding rather than subtracting because it obviates the necessity of taking money away from one employee in order to reward another.

In a company with rather a large number of high-performance employees, it's easy to run through this merit profit-sharing fund very quickly. We use two guides to help keep the playing field level:

1. *Retrospective performance.* We ask ourselves, "If we had known person X was going to be this terrific last year, what would her salary have been? That being the case, what's a fair level of profit sharing on the higher salary?" Using the incremental profit sharing, we do our best to bring the treasured X up to what she really should have made in salary and profit sharing combined—and make a note to adjust her salary at the next convenient opportunity.

2. *Comparative total cash compensation (salary and profit sharing).* As a test of relative fairness, we add the projected profit sharing to the salary of each employee and rank everyone in the company—top to bottom—in declining order of total projected compensation. All employees are thus listed from

most valuable to least, allowing very fine comparisons among people at similar compensation levels. This encourages managers to consider the relative contributions of employees with different skills and helps to maintain fairness among the departments themselves. Who would we rather have in the company, the broadcast buyer who's number 31 on the list or the copywriter who's number 32?

This ranking system also removes the prejudice that can creep in because of the higher luster of some jobs and the low visibility of others. Essentially, the practice of ranking people by value makes senior management look at individuals in a pay cluster comparatively and decide who is contributing more to corporate success. Whatever the judgment, the numbers must confirm it; if not, the managers must honestly face the compensation inequities and tweak the relative shares of profits to keep the final disbursement proportionally fair.

PROFIT SHARING is motivating because money is important to people, and an additional 15 to 50 percent in annual income, delivered in cash, can have a real effect on the quality of an employee's outside life. But as nice as lump-sum payments are, the greater value is the impact profit sharing has on the employees' belief in the fairness of the company the 364 days each year that profits are not distributed.

Open-book financials and universally shared profits convince employees that this company is a good place to spend their careers. Certainly, our best employees could always get other jobs at higher salaries from competitors that operate on the star system. But the smart employees realize that their careers are going to span decades, and that real compensation will be measured by the cumulative return over many years. Fairness in something as basic as compensation will encourage your workforce to understand that your company has other qualities that are worth more than just money.

Underlying the financial benefits of profit sharing is the principle that each person adds value to the company's product, and that each person's incremental contribution to quality is recognized, appreciated, and rewarded. Ownership of the company's products is no longer relegated to that small band of senior, front-line employees involved in design or sales. All the company's products become all the employees' creations, and the pride that this instills throughout their ranks creates a more durable loyalty than would all the cash in Fort Knox. This was demonstrated to me in a way that is as poignant as it is instructive. On days when we have a major new business pitch, I get to the office very early to practice my part aloud in the actual room where the meeting will take place. As I rolled into our shop at five-thirty one presentation morning, I was startled to see our entire maintenance crew there ahead of me, grooming the lawns and virtually polishing the driveway leading to the front door of our estate-based campus. "What's up?" I said to Ian, our facilities director. Ian just smiled. "Jim," he said, "by the time those people drive up our driveway, walk into the building, and make their way down to our presentation room, I want them to already *know* the standards of this company."

Ian and his maintenance crew don't see themselves as a bunch of laborers in the business of mowing lawns and raking leaves. They see themselves as salespeople who are an integral part of an advertising agency, whose job it is to add quality to our company's products.

Before you dismiss the concept of universally shared profits as inappropriate for your company, ask yourself this question: Do the people in your organization think like Ian Hunter?

# 15

# $\mathcal{G}$OALS WITHOUT NUMBERS, POLICIES WITHOUT MANUALS

EVERY GREAT ORGANIZATION must not only identify its long-term goals, it must share those objectives with every person in the company. After all, it's pretty hard for your people to get to where you want them to go if they don't know where they're going. As an advertising person with years of exposure to big business, I can confidently report that a clear philosophic direction is not a great strength of most mature American corporations, nor is it the strength of many smaller ones either.

Scratch the surface of the business plans of 95 percent of either America's largest corporations or its incipient entrepreneurs, and you'll find that long-term goals supporting both types of organizations will be spreadsheets. Lotus 1-2-3 has liberated a generation of companies from the hard work of knowing and articulating the principles for which they stand, and has permitted them to fabricate business sand castles that rival San Simeon. Beware the ubiquitous five-year plan, my son, even more than the Jabberwock and the Frumious Bandersnatch.

Nothing is less likely to influence the future success of any large organization than its recent past, because its primary business decisions will have to be made in response to unknowable shifts in the world economy and unfathomable eruptions on the political landscape. And nothing could be more useless to a young company that's struggling with the elemental problems of survival than a miasma of annual projections subject to the future shrugs of an unpredictable world.

The world is in entropy, with all objects moving toward and away from one another in random directions at random speeds. None of that lovely historical information and orderly spreadsheet data will ground an organization as solidly as clear organizational philosophies, and nothing will help it be successful like a little bit of luck. Ask yourself this: What happened to all those splendid five-year plans that were presented to and swallowed up by America's bankers on October 18, 1987, one day before the stock market imploded?

I believe that for organizations pursuing excellence the four greatest possible wastes of management time are long-term sales and profit projections, regimented departmental budgets, artificial organization charts, and stifling corporate policy manuals. Each teaches employees exactly the opposite of what makes companies great:

~ Five- (and even three-) year projections never come true, because business, like weather, follows the chaos theory: something unanticipated always changes the neat expectations of the normal working environment.

~ Budgets tell employees that the quantification of value is really someone else's decision, even if they are responsible for achieving the results.

~ Organization charts lie to employees and clients alike about who really does what and who really reports to whom.

~ Policy manuals tell employees that it's OK to beat

the system as long as they can find the loopholes in the rules; therefore, policy manuals become the springboards for individual exploitation and the corrupters of organizational evenhandedness.

## MULTI-YEAR PLANS

It's not that we don't create three-year plans—of course we do. Our bank demands it. Therefore, dutifully, we take our current year's figures and, with the magic of Lotus 1-2-3, extend our numbers by some minimal annual growth, say 3 to 5 percent. So as not to thumb our noses at logic, we'll then tweak a few of the numbers that should or shouldn't respond to this linear expansion and—*voilà*—the master plan exists. In my quarter century of dealing with banks, never once has any loan officer used our plan as a retrospective yardstick to measure our agency's success or failure. (Then again, we've always grown by double digits.)

## BUDGETS

Whenever one of our managers suggests that we set up a budget to monitor the activity of some function, I ask, "What if excellence costs more? Should we stop short and settle for mediocrity? Or, if excellence can be achieved less expensively, should we encourage people to think in wasteful terms?" I submit to you that the best budget control an organization can have is an involved, motivated and enfranchised workforce.

Let me illustrate my point. Speculative advertising (work prepared at agency cost during the competitive stage of an account review) is extremely costly—not just in agency man-hours but in research and consumer testing, as well as the materials required for facsimile production of print, radio, and even broadcast campaigns. Creating this speculative work for a major presentation can easily cost upwards of $200,000. No prudent manager would commit to spending such an amount without a statistically reasonable chance of success, as well as an anticipated reward proportional to the risk.

We were aware of the order of magnitude of our risk when we plunged into the BMW pitch. Yet at no time during the process was there a centralized budget. Our research director,

Jim Hartrich, organized his consumer investigations exclusively for their yield of applicable intelligence, not some preordained financial formula. Where he set out personally to interview all 350 BMW dealers, he found that the consistency of information from the first fifty made the rest of the process unnecessary. That saved us money. In contrast, all the highly paid industry consultants we brought on board yielded only droplets of sustained value. Who would have guessed?

Our creative supervisor, Margaret McGovern, spent virtually as much on exquisite illustrations and photo enlargements that we abandoned before the final pitch as she did on those that survived. Only during the final week could the brand team decide which of our proposed directions was the most accurate and the most evocative, and many didn't make the cut. Yet the discarded artwork had done its job: The process of selectivity helped us make the best decisions.

These expenditures were neither indulgences nor careless management—they were prudent decisions that helped us cover all possible bases. Each member of the pitch team spent what was necessary to win BMW, and not a penny more.

Surely, my peers suggest, in a company with $150 million in annual billings, such as Mullen, there has to be some sense of how much each function costs. There is indeed. Since we are exacting in the ways we monitor and categorize all expenses, we know the price of each finite operation for the past dozen years and, cumulatively, the average and annual costs of every category. Our financial analysts use these patterns to assess the risk on projects like new business pitches and to forecast the resulting increases in future expenses.

While we constantly evaluate these numbers in our financial center, we never discuss our cost projections with the people in control of purchasing the goods and services. My fear is that this *a priori* knowledge would set up a predisposition in their minds to meet our corporate forecasts, high or low—an attitude that might directly contradict our best chances for success. Instead, we trust that those responsible will manage prudently for the benefit of our company (their source of stability) and their own self-interest (their profit sharing). Should, someday, a manager trend toward irresponsibility, those around him would take note of his curious decisions and take corrective peer action long before the corporate numbers began to go south.

Budgets inevitably cause people to miss the big picture while looking at details in isolation. They also encourage bad decisions—a tendency to spend too liberally early in the year, and then too cautiously as the money runs out. Worst of all, they prevent good people from performing their jobs—to think about what should be done, then courageously do it. The best budget control any organization can have is a solid, entrepreneurial culture that grounds all employees in the principles of rights and responsibilities, financials open for all to see, and the chance for each person to share in the profits.

## ORGANIZATION CHARTS

Please raise your right hand and repeat after me: "I will never, *never* create an organization chart of my company or group, and I will never let any of my colleagues do so either."

The nature of organizational responsibilities is far too fluid and dynamic ever to be captured on a matrix of orderly arranged boxes, or defined by a network of connecting lines. Organizations are living things whose components change constantly, becoming more or less important according to the circumstances of the moment. Therefore, all those horizontally arranged management squares are, in fact, constantly migrating up and down in sympathy with the momentary importance of each job, the momentary activeness of a specific problem or opportunity, and the disparate capabilities of the individuals those boxes represent.

Worse yet, should you ever attempt to force an organization to operate day to day strictly obeying the chart's vertical reporting structure, the work output would slow to a crawl. The reporting lines of real-life systems look more like sea urchins than right-angle arrows. Influences extend in many directions and are received from many sources. Sure, a few main two-way channels define each person's basic sense of hierarchical rights and responsibilities, but to insist that these channels are exclusive is plain nonsense. Tell people to whom they report and who reports to them, then let everyone figure out how best to use the system to get things done.

## POLICY MANUALS

Policy manuals pretend to be arbiters of evenhandedness, but actually they are its corrupters. Think about it. The power to decide what is fair both for the individual and the organization is removed from the hands of an on-the-spot manager, a person who is capable of making a reasoned judgment, and transferred to a book written years before by someone who is (or who thinks like) a lawyer.

These compendiums of the four thousand things each employee must do every day and the forty thousand each may never do are terribly destructive. In practice, they are a playground for every person who wants to find a loophole that allows him to take advantage of the organization. Ironically, policy manuals tend to organize the rules so that your best and most entrepreneurial people will be the first to ferret out the system's cracks. Perhaps the most corrosive effect of policy manuals is that they treat every person and every circumstance in the same way, which is absurd. If circumstances are all individual, why shouldn't the policies governing them be equally customized? An accommodation made for a great employee does not become the right of another who's marginal.

Certainly, every organization needs *a few* guidelines—vacation, bereavement leave, and so on. But if it's more than a few, it's too many. Those few fixed corporate policies should serve primarily as bulwarks against a potential exploiter, not rigid regulations applied without judgment. For instance, we publish a policy allowing five sick days with pay, but make it clear that the concept of sick days is not interchangeable with the concept of holidays. Because our people do not exploit their sick days, managers feel comfortable making exceptions when good employees' illnesses extend beyond the canonical limit.

The ultimate problem with policy manuals is that they waste valuable employee time. The more comprehensive they attempt to be, the greater the opportunity for debate and disagreement. Remember, every nanosecond an employee spends on internal machinations—interpreting the fine print of policy manuals, or worrying about the security of his job or how to handle office politics, or wondering if his compensation is fair—he isn't thinking about your clients' businesses.

## LONG-TERM GOALS

The purpose of long-term goals is to get the entire employee body shambling down the same road at more or less the same pace, without individuals or groups leaping ahead, lagging behind, or wandering afield. Moreover, if the long-term goals also have the effect of eliminating the roadblocks and smoothing the path, that employee community can get pretty far down that path together, and do so at an impressive pace.

Most business executives establish quantitative long term goals. By contrast, I believe that if a company is able to grow its competency each year, numerical success will inexorably follow. Therefore, it's the leader's job to establish goals for her company that will enhance the *quality* of the organization, and this means improving the quality of employees' personal lives.

Long-term goals aren't your company's financial wish list, they're its principles, and a company's principles are its main engines of growth. Our agency's policy manual, *Philosophies, Goals and Promises*, is nothing more than a pragmatic enhancement of our company's long-term goals. It is my contention that, if we can articulate the reasoning behind the company's business objectives, our employees will intelligently pursue their work in ways that are equally fair to the organization, their colleagues, and themselves.

I wrote our long-term goals in 1975, and I've never seen any reason to change them. With a new word here and there and a bit of intelligent customizing, I'd bet that they would work for a large number of businesses that have nothing to do with advertising.

# MULLEN'S LONG TERM GOALS:

1. *Create a balanced team that produces consistent, high-quality products.*

    ~ Attract the best people for every position.

    ~ Understand each job in the company, and understand its value to you and the company.

    ~ Treat each person and every job function with respect.

    ~ Create quality at every level, in every product detail.

2. *Create an environment that fosters personal and professional growth.*

    ~ Decentralize authority: give good people the responsibility to get the job done and the rights to do the job well—then get out of their way.

    ~ Recognize and accommodate individual growth.

3. *Create an environment that's honest, productive, friendly and fun.*

    ~ Create jobs that match people's strengths.

    ~ Respect the personal rights of your colleagues.

~ Be tolerant of others' personalities and their quirks.

~ Don't be greedy. Avoid politics.

~ Don't be greedy. Avoid politics.

4. *Grow fast enough to compete with the best agencies for major brand name clients.*

~ Grow the company fast enough to match the growth of the talented people.

~ Grow coherently—don't throw away the entrepreneurial qualities that got us where we are.

~ Grow into major accounts—so that we have the scope to show how good we really are. We want to compete against the varsity.

5. *Build a national reputation for great work.*

~ Our future employees should know us for great creative. Therefore, publicize our best creative ideas in national awards shows and in the ad trade press.

~ Our prospective clients should know us as brand builders. Therefore, promote our high-visibility accounts in the national business press.

~ Our peers should know us as winners. Therefore,

make the public aware of our business practices, our
results, and our unique facility.

6. *Provide the best compensation programs in the American advertising industry.*

~ Salaries that match those of the best, large agencies, since they are our *real* competitors. Mullen salaries should be plus or minus 20 percent of a top
competitive scale, allowing for differences in talent
and experience but recognizing the innate value of
each position.

~ Structured profit sharing programs that distribute a
substantial share of the agency's net income to all
employees.

~ Significant equity participation for each long-term
employee through a cost-free stock ownership program (ESOP).

~ Annual nonqualified stock programs for officers and
key employees.

As you can see for yourself, we have never had a quantitative goal in the history of our company. Yet our growth is the

envy of our industry; our profits always remain at or above those of the top third of our peers; and we are consistently among the agencies most awarded for creative excellence.

Maybe these creative and financial results have nothing to do with the communal philosophies we express as our Long Term Goals. But I bet you wouldn't have much luck convincing our employees of that.

# 16

## *M*ANAGEMENT:
## THE ILLUSION OF POWER

IN ROMAN TIMES, each conquering general who paraded his captives and loot through the city was provided with his own government-issue slave. As the hero basked in the crowd's cheers, the slave stood behind him and whispered incessantly into his ear, *"Sic transit gloria mundi"*—roughly translated as "How fleeting is our glory." I am reminded of that warning each day as I ascend the stairs to my agency corner office, confronted by one almightily sobering thought: "It is fortunate I am protected by the august title of president of this company, because I am demonstrably unqualified to be anything else."

The day I founded the agency (in 1970, on April Fool's

Day, of course), I was one person standing alone in my two-room apartment. Since no one else was present to disagree, I summarily anointed myself president. That's turned out to have been one of the best business decisions I ever made! Not only, as a friend once said, is president the only title in an ad agency that a mother can understand, president remains the only job in the company I have been consistently qualified to do. Today, if I were to apply to any of our departments under a pseudonym, my letter and résumé wouldn't make it past the directors' administrative assistants. In every department at every level of our agency, across a wide range of skills, there are people whose expertise simply overwhelms my own.

Twenty-five years ago I was the jack of all trades because there was no one else on whom I could call for help. Then I hired to get some relief from a blizzard of obligations; today I'm in full retreat from most of our agency's substantive involvements.

First, Jeanne Ridgway came along with her calculator and razor-sharp mind. Good. I didn't have to balance the books anymore. Then Steve Haesche joined as our first real art director. Well, that was fine—after all, I could still write. About the same time, Paul Silverman hit his stride as a copywriter and rapidly demonstrated his superiority in this craft. OK, no prob-lem, I still knew about production. Oops, Vivian Christiano appeared, and she understood more about the nuances of slid dots than I did about dotted i's. Hmm, was I running out of places in the agency where I could hide? My final camouflage disappeared when Joe Grimaldi walked in the door. It was clear from the outset that Joe was the better strategist and organizer. Ultimately and deservedly, Joe agreed to become the agency's chief operating officer. That does it, I thought. The jig is up. I'm without a job!

Ultimately, of course, truth dawned. None of these func-tions was my most important job, and none of them ever had been. As replaceable as I proved to be in the operations of our company, I still had the unique opportunity to influence the quality of every piece of work we created as well as the quality of every client relationship we formed. While my business card identified me as president, it didn't really begin to describe what I did. Slowly, I figured out that I really ran a department, one that was even more basic to our company's existence than those of Creative, Account Services, and Production.

In actual practice, I was the head of the Department of

Environment and Standards: It was my responsibility to define the very soul of our agency.

I submit to you that, to some degree, every manager in every business has two jobs: one stated on a business card, another that is unexpressed but much more important. While the president may be the ultimate director of Environment and Standards, every manager in the company is a part of that group and, therefore, responsible for implementing the organization's critical philosophies. In addition to each manager's substantive obligations, he must help create a business culture that catalyzes the productivity and happiness of the workforce and an environment that is accountable for each employee's success.

The greatest illusion in business is that employees work for managers; this, of course, is exactly the inverse of reality. Look at an organization hard and the truth is inescapable: All managers, in fact, work for employees. As the unions learned in the 1920s, the day that a significant group of employees chooses to stop working, managers are helpless to carry out the tasks of business.

Every day, the workforce arrives at your doorstep primed to observe how you teach and implement the corporate culture and to measure how you exercise the standards your organization purports to honor. If they believe in your leadership, they reward you with superior efforts. If you fail their expectations, they punish you with substandard quality and efficiency. All in all, a workforce's productivity is a fair measure of how employees rate a manager's performance.

If you accept this premise, then you also will recognize that managers are primarily in the teaching business and only secondarily in the managing business. Every philosophy, attitude, and business practice used by a manager in dealing with his employees ultimately will be re-expressed by the employees through the quality of their work. Show me an organization with a high absentee rate, problems with expense accounts, or a cover-your-butt mentality, and I'll show you a manager who is secretly leading the pack in every one of those deficiencies. Directly or indirectly, the philosophies, attitudes, and practices of each of the company's managers find their way to that company's customers, through either the quality of the products delivered or the nature of the relationships sustained. Managers reap what they sow, sweet and sour.

Some years back, I had a conversation with Jay Chiat, the

legendary founder of America's most honored advertising agency. "You know," Jay said, "other agencies constantly contact our hottest young stars and seduce them away with huge salaries and lots of fanfare in the trade press. Yet, a year or two later, it's like these young stars just disappeared off the face of the earth." When Jay's competitors hired his hotshots, the qualities they couldn't buy and didn't get were Chiat/Day's fertile environment and the support of the hundreds of talented colleagues that make each creative person's work so great.

Jay's point applies to all businesses. Great work doesn't just spring from the minds of one or two creative people. It is actually produced by an entire organization that understands and encourages that greatness.

Great environments cannot be created by fiat. They are built cumulatively by every manager in the organization, bit by bit, over time, by hundreds of thousands of day-to-day events—every hello, every hallway conversation, every memo, every decision, and every interaction with every employee in the organization. One of the great myths of management is that employees really are influenced by our memos and speeches. More often than not, those magnificent statements given at moments of great triumph or disaster are so transparently self-promotional that employees are more likely to receive them skeptically than be moved to action.

I believe that a manager's best-remembered teachings come at unexpected times—a compassionate hand on a shoulder; a supportive comment when the politically safe course is silence; a word of encouragement when criticism might easily be justified; a selfless distribution of credit in front of people who make a difference.

When all is said and done, managers influence their employees less by what they say than by what they do. Yet, day in and day out, managers nick, dent and trample on the very same standards that they demand their employees observe, blithely excusing themselves from the same policies they inflict on others. The fact that managers can transgress the organization's ethics and seem to get away with it doesn't mean that they're not observed and that they don't pay a price. In fact, their deeds are seen by all. Their motives are transparent and the results are disastrous. By their actions, they have just delivered instructions to all around them that the real organizational standards are not honesty, integrity, professionalism and fairness; rather, they are power, insincerity, duplicity and fraud.

Standards have to be clear and they have to be observed by all, regardless of title, rank or longevity. Lots of companies are good at identifying and enforcing measurables—but often the wrong kind. Ask most managers about the standards of their organizations and they'll recite statistics on productivity and efficiency. Now, far be it from me to suggest that numerical measurements are unimportant, but they are only capable of *defining* situations, not *influencing* them. The standards that really drive efficiency and productivity are philosophical and, therefore, immeasurable. Yet, these corporate philosophies are the very engines that encourage employees to perform at their highest levels.

*The most important standards in an organization are those that account for fairness, respect, care, honesty, integrity and fun!*

I don't doubt for a minute the basic morality of the vast majority of American companies. In my experience, business (even the advertising business) remains quite untainted by those kinds of wholesale ethical abuses illustrated in Hollywood's venomous portrayals of corporate life. For every news headline that unearths some odoriferous business deal, millions of commercial agreements are struck daily by irreproachably honest people doing their best to do good things. In real-life business the corrosive flaws are less a matter of overt dishonesty (like cheating and stealing) and more a tendency to soften ethical edges. The most damaging attacks on standards aren't the work of opportunistic rascals. Rather, they spring more frequently and more dangerously from a thousand minor infractions committed or permitted by ordinary managers pursuing business as they have come to know it.

It is insidious how often the powerful incentive of self-preservation will slither into your organizational Eden to suggest an insignificant little compromise—sacrificing product integrity for money, shading employee fairness to accommodate an expediency, or allowing a financially helpful but draining customer relationship to invade and degrade business standards. Compromises are like drugs; immediately rewarding, ultimately dangerous. Never forget that your employees pay you that prominent executive salary to be on guard against the viruses of compromise.

Any organization can hire clerks to administer its quantitative standards, but for the more critical qualitative standards it must rely on its managers' judgments and the unwavering application of its organizational philosophies. The only sure way to apply these safeguards is to operate on the principle that everyone knows everything (as usually they do) and that every exercise of standards will be observed, weighed, and evaluated by your employees (as always they will). If you are not comfortable with the thought of posting each of your decisions on the company bulletin board without a long explanation, then odds are your actions are indefensible and ought to be reconsidered. Freedom, after all, is simply being able to live with the consequences of your decisions.

Now, no manager walks through the front door and says to himself, "Well, I elevated a few standards yesterday, time now to build a little environment." You build your environment and promulgate your standards as you go about your everyday tasks. As each employee learns and applies these principles every day, you'll experience the thrill of watching your business philosophies emerging as organizational operating practices.

Still, I would be less than honest if I did not spend at least a sentence or two cautioning you on the darker side of business building. Many, many times in my life I internally concluded that the pain of leadership is not always worth its rewards. Yet, like a drug, it is so addictive that there is a point at which it becomes impossible to live without its rush. It turns out that what fuels the entrepreneurial obsession, what motivates financially maxed-out leaders to continue building an already successful company, isn't more money, power, and fame. It is a process that becomes so obsessive and so much fun that nothing else can take its place. The details of operations fill the manager's mind every waking moment; the organization's value dominates his thoughts and looms as the most important thing in the world. The leader and the entity become indistinguishable. The organization not only reflects the leader's vision, it becomes his life.

When I first went into business for myself, I recall telling my wife, "This is for us—so we can have more time together." What naïveté! Within six months, I had learned that the creation of the agency wasn't for "us" at all, it was for me. Moreover, my obsession caused me to focus so exclusively on business-building for so many years that, micron by micron, that marriage evaporated into the ethers. Please don't let it happen to you.

The poet, writer, artist, and humorist James Thurber commented on the transcendental rewards of leadership with mischievous elegance:

> *"The world is so full of a number of things,*
> *I am sure we should all be happy as kings,*
> *And you know how happy kings are."*

My bet is that even Mozart died feeling that his most magnificent work was less than his beginning vision. Satisfaction is the most transitory of all emotions.

But if satisfaction is elusive, what *is* leadership's lasting pleasure? Pride—pride in the work, pride in the people, pride in the inherent goodness of the organization whose values you espouse and share. Pride is a deep and enduring emotion. While satisfaction is ephemeral, pride will stay with you throughout the vagaries of business cycles. Like a stone in water, pride becomes more smoothed and polished by time. In your knowing heart, an appreciation develops for the wonder of what you have helped create, and remains strong regardless of the uninformed observations of both critics and admirers.

For me, leading—building and managing—is like the pursuit of world records. Once runners thought the four-minute mile was an impenetrable wall. But when the four-minute barrier finally tumbled and that psychological impediment was removed, the record kept dropping, level after level, to a time once thought not humanly achievable. And every runner knows that it will fall again.

Arne Naess made a poignant observation after he climbed Mt. Everest. "I had a dream. I reached it. I lost the dream, and I miss it." In business we are blessed. There is always a higher mountain on the horizon.

# 17

# $\mathcal{W}$HITHER BOUND?
## PERSPECTIVES ON THE FUTURE

THE CARIBBEAN OF the sixties was a languorous and lovely place with only a veneer of governmental formality, and that seemingly handed down intact from its eighteenth-century European colonizers. Upon making landfall at a port with links to the British Commonwealth, each charter yacht captain was required to complete a centuries-old form with particulars of his boat, his crew, and his sailing intentions. The final question was phrased in an arcane form of English left over from the era when Nelson's fleet plied the same waters. "Whither bound?" it poignantly asked, and that question always made me pause and wonder.

"Whither bound?" The obvious answer was, of course, the

name of the next outward-bound island as the yacht threaded its way through the chain of archipelagoes. But somehow, the query taunted me to consider not only the next day's island, but life's next port of call. Time has never truly silenced that question. In a sense, I suppose I have spent my life trying to respond.

Today, Mullen is a company that has gained a modicum of size, success, and recognition. Quantified, we look pretty good—hundreds of millions of dollars, hundreds of people, much awarded, very profitable. But, by the standards posed at the beginning of this book, are we really a great company? Not yet, I'm afraid—certainly not all the time or among all of the people whose respect would indicate that we are getting there.

It isn't that I demand a perfect report card on our agency from every constituency. Kai Fuwa, a senior scientist at the biophysics lab, used to say, "The data don't have to be perfect, Jim, just reasonable." Still, I remain sadly aware that our agency's reputation is strong from a narrow segment of our natural market. Can we be considered a great company if most of America's senior advertisers have never even heard of us? Is our middle management prepared to become the new pillars of our culture? Do our younger people really understand and believe in all the ideals that I've urged you to embrace?

Now that I'm through haranguing you about being productive leaders, it is time for me to turn up the pressure on myself. Using the tools I believe in so deeply, I will rejoin my colleagues in their fight to continue to build an organization with the values we treasure:

1. A great company
2. with happy people
3. producing a great product
4. together.

Will you, I, or any of us ever get to the end of this adventure? Will we indeed create even a modicum of greatness, or are we, like the crew of the Flying Dutchman, destined to sail forever on challenging seas? Who knows—maybe not, but probably.

Yet I have learned from the journey so far that the reward is not in reaching the destination but with what art the vessel challenges the opposing elements. Well sailed, the search for greatness is a voyage worth taking, whether you're starting up the next General Motors or struggling to bring fundamental change to one of GM's departments today.

WHEN I FIRST arrived in the Caribbean in 1964, the original wave of charter skippers was feeling threatened by encroaching civilization and they were preparing to follow the sun west toward Micronesia. "But before I leave," said one, "I need to spend the year painting my boat." For others it was "I'll go as soon as I rebuild my engine," or "Just a couple more charters so I can buy better sails." They all seemed to have reasons—good reasons—to delay the trip one additional season. As time passed, I noticed that boats got painted, engines fixed, and sails renewed. But when I left the Caribbean in 1967, most of these same yachts and skippers were still swinging listlessly on their moorings.

"If only they knew how easy it is," said my boat owner and friend Sid Miller. "You just pull up the anchor—and go."

My anchor is aweigh. Yours?